GCSE Maths In A Week Foundation Tier For the Grade 9-1 Exams

www.How2Become.com

As part of this product you have also received FREE access to online tests that will help you to pass GCSE Maths assessments.

To gain access, simply go to:

www.MyEducationalTests.co.uk

Get more products for passing any test at:

www.How2Become.com

Orders: Please contact How2Become Ltd, Suite 3, 40 Churchill Square Business Centre, Kings Hill, Kent ME19 4YU.

You can order through Amazon.co.uk under ISBN: **9781912370238**, via the website www.How2Become.com or through Gardners.com.

ISBN: **9781912370238**

First published in 2018 by How2Become Ltd.

Typeset by Katie Noakes for How2Become Ltd.

Disclaimer

Every effort has been made to ensure that the information contained within this guide is accurate at the time of publication. How2Become Ltd is not responsible for anyone failing any part of any selection process as a result of the information contained within this guide. How2Become Ltd and their authors cannot accept any responsibility for any errors or omissions within this guide, however caused. No responsibility for loss or damage occasioned by any person acting, or refraining from action, as a result of the material in this publication can be accepted by How2Become Ltd.

The information within this guide does not represent the views of any third party service or organisation.

Contains public sector information licensed under the Open Government Licence v3.0.

CONTENTS

HOW TO USE THIS GUIDE

This guide comprises a full breakdown of the GCSE Maths exam for the Maths Foundation Tier.

Not only have we provided you with a rundown of what to expect, how to prepare, and top tips for students and parents, but this book will help you to tailor your revision in just 7 days!

Take a look at the below structure to get an idea about how this guide will be formatted:

GCSE Maths Prep
A Chapter Full of Tips

NUMBERS
Rounding and Estimating
Multiples, Factors, and Primes
Fractions, Decimals, and Percentages
Indices
Standard Form
Surds

RATIO, PROPORTION, AND RATES OF CHANGE
Ratio
Percentages
Direct Proportion
Indirect Proportion

DAY 3

GEOMETRY AND MEASURES
Angles and Lines
Loci and Constructions
Circles, Sectors, and Arcs
Pythagoras' Theorem
Units of Measure
Trigonometry and Vectors

DAY 4

PROBABILITY AND STATISTICS
Probability
Collecting and Representing Data
Analysing Data

DAY 5

ALGEBRA
Expressions and Formulae
Linear and Simultaneous Equations
Quadratic Equations
Inequalities
Sequences
Graphs

DAY 6

Exam Practice
Numbers
Ratio, Proportion, and Rates of Change
Geometry and Measures
Probability and Statistics
Algebra
Problem Solving

DAY 7

<u>Exam Practice</u>
Numbers
Ratio, Proportion, and Rates of Change
Geometry and Measures
Probability and Statistics
Algebra
Problem Solving

By following this 7-day plan, you will be able to work through your GCSE Maths revision in a clear, easy-to-follow format.

Whether you have left your revision to the last minute, or you simply want to brush up on all of your knowledge in the last week prior to the exam, this guide is the ideal resource for you. It will help you to fully comprehend the contents of your GCSE Maths exam, and hopefully pass with top marks!

GCSE MATHS PREP

GCSE MATHS EXAM STRUCTURE

Your GCSE Maths (Foundation) examination is comprised of **three** sections:

Paper 1: Non-Calculator

Marks out of 80

1 hour and 30 minutes

33.3% of GCSE

Paper 2: Calculator

Marks out of 80

1 hour and 30 minutes

33.3% of GCSE

Paper 3: Calculator

Marks out of 80

1 hour and 30 minutes

33.3% of GCSE

Assessment Objectives

AO1 (50%) = Use and apply standard techniques. Students should be able to:

- Accurately recall facts, terminology and definitions;
- Use and interpret notation correctly;
- Accurately carry out routine procedures or set tasks requiring multi-step solutions.

AO2 (25%) = Reason, interpret, and communicate effectively.

Students should be able to:

- Make deductions, inferences and draw conclusions from mathematical information;

- Construct chains of reasoning to achieve a given result;

- Interpret and communicate information accurately;

- Present arguments and proofs ;

- Assess the validity of an argument and critically evaluate a given way of presenting information.

AO3 (25%) = Solve problems within mathematics and in other contexts. Students should be able to:

- Translate problems in mathematical or non-mathematical contexts into a process or a series of mathematical processes;

- Make and use connections between different parts of mathematics;

- Interpret results in the context of the given problem;

- Evaluate methods used and results obtained;

- Evaluate solutions to identify how they may have been affected by assumptions made.

Breakdown of GCSE Maths topics

The content for the GCSE Maths exam is broken down into the following five areas:

- Numbers;

- Ratio, Proportion, and Rates of Change;

- Geometry and Measures;

- Probability and Statistics;

- Algebra.

Please note:

In this guide, we have also included a section on problem solving, just to give students the chance to further their analytical skills with regards to mathematical concepts.

Below we have outlined the weighting of each topic area:

Topic Area	Foundation Tier Weighting (%)
Numbers	25%
Ratio, Proportion, and Rates of Change	25%
Geometry and Measures	15%
Probability and Statistics	15%
Algebra	20%

A CHAPTER FULL OF TIPS

Not only do we think it's important to learn about the structure and content of your exam, but we also think it practical that you revise some top tips and soak up some of the best exam advice prior to commencing your revision.

Tip 1 – Find out as much as you can!

Before your exam, you should find out as much information as you can about what you'll face on the day.

Below are some of the most essential things that you SHOULD know before undergoing your revision:

- The examination board;

- The subject content;

- The books to be focusing on;

- Understanding how much each section is worth (in percentage).

Tip 2 – Create a timetable

It is important that every minute leading up to your exam is spent wisely and effectively.

The best way to do this is to create a timetable for yourself and try to adhere to it as much as possible.

On the following page, we have created a sample timetable that you can fill out according to your Maths exam.

REVISION TIMETABLE

Week Beginning: _____

	Monday	Tuesday	Wednesday	Thursday	Friday	Saturday	Sunday
9am							
10am							
11am							
12 noon							
1pm							
2pm							
3pm							
4pm							
5pm							
6pm							
7pm							
8pm							

*You will need to fill in this timetable for every week leading up to your exams. Once you sit an exam, you can take that out of your timetable, and spend more time on something else.

REVISION TIMETABLE

Week Beginning: _____

	Monday	Tuesday	Wednesday	Thursday	Friday	Saturday	Sunday
9am							
10am							
11am							
12 noon							
1pm							
2pm							
3pm							
4pm							
5pm							
6pm							
7pm							
8pm							

*You will need to fill in this timetable for every week leading up to your exams. Once you sit an exam, you can take that out of your timetable, and spend more time on something else.

Tip 3 – Prepare for your exam as early as possible

You can make your life so much easier by preparing for your GCSEs in advance. By preparing early, you will be able to overcome exam nerves and stress, therefore improving your overall performance when it comes to the real exam.

Tip 4 – Give yourself enough time

You should begin revising 6-8 weeks prior to your GCSEs. Although you can still achieve high scores if you revise later than this, you won't be able to guarantee your best results.

Tip 5 – Organisation is key

When it comes to exams, the majority of students will have to organise their time sufficiently in order to make the most out of their learning.

Students will likely be facing numerous exams across a short period. Therefore, they need to be able to break up their revision and set aside time for each subject.

Tip 6 – The night before your exam...

The night before the exam, you should STOP revising. If you continue revising the night before, you will do yourself no favours. You will feel more stressed, more pressured and more tired – none of which will help your performance.

THINGS TO CONSIDER

The night before the exam:

- Ensure that you have all of the equipment you need for your exam (pens, pencils, rubbers, protractors, rulers, etc.);

- Double check your exam timetable so that you know what the start time is and where the exam is being held;

- Have a relaxing bath, and try not to think about the exam;

- Try to get an early night. This will allow you to wake up feeling refreshed and ready to go!

Tip 7 – In your exam...

Whilst your brain will be focused on trying to remember everything you have learned in the last few weeks, there are a few things you need to be aware of.

LISTEN!

An invigilator will start the exam by running through the exam procedures. Pay attention to what the invigilator is saying, as this may answer some of the questions or queries you have about the exam.

When invited to do so, you will need to fill in the front of your examination booklet. The front of your examination paper contains lots of information which you need to read carefully.

INSTRUCTIONS TO CANDIDATES:

- Before you begin filling in the front of your examination booklet, make sure that you have the correct testing paper in front of you:

  o Make sure that the paper is for the correct subject (i.e. GCSE Mathematics);

  o Make sure that you are sitting the correct tier (i.e. foundation or higher);

  o Make sure you have all of the papers required for the exam (i.e. Non-Calculator, Calculator, Formula Sheet).

- Fill in ALL of your details on the front of your examination booklet. This will usually consist of the following:

- o Surname;
- o First Name/s;
- o Candidate Signature;
- o Candidate Number (this will be provided to you on the day);
- o Centre Name and Number (this will be provided to you on the day).

- Answer ALL of the questions in the spaces provided;

- When it comes to calculations, make sure you show ALL of your working out;

- If you have any questions, please raise your hand and wait for someone to assist.

ACTION CHECKLIST!

- Work through the paper at a steady pace;

- If you have any questions about the exam, be sure to raise your hand and wait for someone to assist you;

- Make sure you have all of the correct equipment (rulers etc.);

- Don't spend too long on one question;

- If you have time at the end, go back through the paper and check your work.

Tip 8 – After your exam...

AFTER YOUR EXAM, DO:

✓ Reward yourself with some free time. Even if you have other exams coming up, you should spend some time doing something you enjoy. Just relax!

✓ Forget about the exam. It's over. There is no point dwelling about what you could have done, or what you didn't do.

✓ Be positive and proud. If you put that extra time and hard work into preparing for your exam, then you have done your best, and that's all you can do.

AFTER YOUR EXAM, DON'T:

× Do a post-mortem of your exam. Do not pick your exam apart. Do not think about the 'what ifs'. The exam is over. You cannot change anything now, so try not to worry.

× Discuss the exam with your friends. Discussing the exam and then thinking 'I didn't write that' or 'I should have done that', will make you feel disheartened. Try to avoid any conversation about the contents of the exam.

× Worry yourself. Everyone comes out of exams fearing the worst. This is a common feeling amongst students, the chances are you are worrying over nothing.

× Feel upset or disheartened if the exam didn't go according to plan. There are several opportunities for re-sits, and who knows, you may have done better than expected!

Prepare! Practice! Persevere!

Tip 9 – Use our revision guides

Here at How2Become, we have a range of GCSE Maths resources to help you on your way to securing top marks.

GCSE Maths is Easy: the ultimate guide for anyone who finds mathematics challenging. This exciting guide is filled with fun and interesting facts to help you understand maths in a way that makes it more compelling to learn, and more importantly, easier to understand!

GCSE Maths is Easy: Practice Papers - Foundation Tier Sets 1 & 2 is the ultimate new resource on the market to ensure you get the best preparation for your GCSE Maths and achieve a high grade. This unique practice book contains 2 × full mock exams for the higher level papers (2 × Non-Calculator Papers and 2 × Calculator papers).

GCSE Maths in a Week: Higher Tier is the ultimate practice resource for those wanting to pass GCSE maths the easy way. This guide is designed to make maths fun – using fascinating facts and real-life scenarios, this guide is sure to make an impression on your learning.

GCSE Maths is Easy: Practice Papers - Higher Tier Sets 1 & 2 is the ultimate new resource on the market to ensure you get the best preparation for your GCSE Maths and achieve a high grade. This unique practice book contains 2 × full mock exams for the higher level papers (2 × Non-Calculator Papers and 2 × Calculator papers).

GCSE Maths is Easy: Higher Tier is the ultimate practice resource for those wanting to pass GCSE maths the easy way. This guide is designed to make maths fun. Using fascinating facts and real-life scenarios, this guide is sure to make an impression on your learning.

SEARCH THE SYMBOL

Press this button FIRST if you want to use something written above a button.

E.g. (Shift) + (=) will give you (%)

To square a number push this button.

For a fraction, press the first number followed by this button and then the next number (to form your fraction).

You may need to press the (shift) button first.

(STO, RCL & M+)

If you are working out multiple calculations, and you need to remember the first answer, you can move on to the next calculation and then push this button to add, subtract etc.

Press (shift) and (Π). This is equivalent to the number 3.141...

Use brackets if you are doing multiple operations.

(i.e. important in BIDMAS)

+	ADDITION
−	SUBTRACTION
×	MULTIPLICATION
÷	DIVISION
=	EQUALS
≠	NOT EQUAL
≈	EQUALS APPROXIMATELY
≡	IDENTICAL TO
<	LESS THAN
≤	LESS THAN OR EQUAL TO
>	MORE THAN
≥	MORE THAN OR EQUAL TO
Ø	NULL
%	PERCENTAGE
.	DECIMAL
$^a/_b$	FRACTION
( )	PARENTHESIS (BRACKETS)
x	UNKNOWN VARIABLE
$\propto$	DIRECT PROPORTION
$b \propto {}^1/_m$	INVERSE PROPORTION
∞	INFINITE
$\rightrightarrows$	PARALLEL LINES
A^b	INDICES
a^2	SQUARED
a^3	CUBED
a^5	TO THE POWER 5
$\angle$	ANGLE
$a \times 10^n$	STANDARD FORM

Σ	SUM OF
$\sqrt{}$	SQUARE ROOT
$\sqrt[3]{}$	CUBE ROOT
$\llcorner$	RIGHT ANGLE
$\cap$	INTERSECTION
$\cup$	UNION
π	PI
$\circ$	DEGREE
$\therefore$	THEREFORE
$\perp$	PERPENDICULAR

GCSE REFRESHER

B.I.D.M.A.S

BIDMAS is an acrostic which can be used to remember how you should go about solving maths questions.

BIDMAS is a great way to remember which order you should work out operations, in a calculation that has more than one operation.

The order of operations is as follows:

Brackets ( )

Indices X^2

Division ÷

Multiplication ×

Addition +

Subtraction -

Using BIDMAS, work out the following calculation:

$$8 + 4 \times 3 - 6$$

How to work it out:

- Remember the order of operations.
- In this calculation, you have addition, multiplication, and subtraction.

$8 + 4 \times 3 - 6$

$= 8 + 12 - 6$

$= 20 - 6$

$= 14$

WHOLE NUMBERS

When it comes to whole numbers, you can place these digits under headings. These are called

PLACE VALUE HEADINGS.

Place value headings allow you to work out what each number represents. Whether its hundreds, thousands, millions and so forth.

Below we have created the place value columns which you MUST learn.

Millions	Hundred thousands	Ten thousands	Thousands	Hundreds	Tens	Units
4	5	8	1	2	3	6

As you can see, the above number is broken down into columns. These columns help you work out what each number stands for.

Let's break this number down even further!

4 000 000 = 4 million

500 000 = 5 hundred thousand

80 000 = 80 thousand

1 000 = 1 thousand

200 = 2 hundred

30 = 3 tens (thirty)

6 = 6 units

To break down the number, begin on the right side. Moving left, put a comma after every 3 digits. This will help you to read the number.

4,581,236

So, this number is four million, five hundred and eighty one thousand, two hundred and thirty six.

PLACE VALUES FOR DECIMAL POINTS

When it comes to decimals, you can also place these under columns. The most important thing about decimals is the DECIMAL POINT.

When working with more than one decimal, you must remember to line up the decimal points to be able to compare them correctly.

Below we have created the place value columns which you must learn, and have presented them with an example number.

HUNDREDS	TENS	UNITS	DECIMAL POINT	TENTHS	HUNDREDTHS	THOUSANDTHS
2	8	7	.	1	3	5

As you can see, the above number is broken down into columns. These columns help you work out what each number stands for.

Let's break this number down even further!

200.000 = 2 hundred

80.000 = 8 tens (eighty)

7.000 = 7 units

0.100 = 1 tenth

0.030 = 3 hundredths

0.005 = 5 thousandths

> Remember to always line up the decimal points!
>
> This is particularly important when you are working with multiple decimals.

So, this number would read as two hundred and eighty seven POINT one three five.

DECIMALS

Like fractions, decimals are another way of writing a number that is not whole.

A decimal is in fact 'in-between whole numbers'.

6.48 ⟶ This is in between the number 6 and the number 7.

USING PLACE VALUES

In order to work out what the decimal is representing, you should use place values.

These include: units, tenths, hundredths and thousandths.

ADDING AND SUBTRACTING DECIMALS

0.5 + 0.62

How to work it out:

```
  0.5
+ 0.62
_____
  1.12
```

The decimal points need to be lined up!

Your answer should begin by adding the decimal point in first, and then add up the columns from right to left.

2.46 - 1.35

How to work it out:

$$
\begin{array}{r}
2.46 \\
- \ 1.35 \\
\hline
1.11 \\
\end{array}
$$

The decimal points need to be lined up!

Your answer should begin by adding the decimal point in first, and then subtracting the columns from right to left.

MULTIPLYING AND DIVIDING DECIMALS

2.5 × 0.2

How to work it out:

- Remove the decimal points.

    25 × 2 = 50

- Now add in the decimal points. **REMEMBER**, you need to work out how many numbers come **AFTER** the decimal point in the question.

- You should notice that two numbers come after the decimal point (the .5 and the .2).

- Therefore 2 numbers need to come after the decimal point in the answer.

    25 × 2 = 50

- So the answer would be 0.50 or 0.5. It is usually written 0.5 (the 0 at the end is not necessary).

REMEMBER: division is easy if you are dividing by whole numbers. You need to move the decimal points in both numbers the same number of places.

5.39 ÷ 1.1

How to work it out:

Move the decimal point 1 space.

53.9 ÷ 11.

• Now ignore the decimal point in 53.9, do long division and then add it in at the end.

```
      049
11 | 539
      5
      0
      53
      44
      99
      99
      00
```

Put the decimal point in the answer directly above the decimal point in the question.

```
      04.9
11 | 53.9
```

ANSWER = 4.9

RECURRING DECIMALS

A recurring decimal is a decimal that goes on forever. For example, 0.4̇ means 0.444444.....

If two dots are used, this shows the beginning and the end of the recurring numbers. For example 0.6̇1̇3 means 0.613613613...

DECIMAL PLACES

Sometimes, instead of rounding off to the nearest whole number, you may be required to round off to the nearest decimal place.

The following rules should ALWAYS be remembered:

- 5 or more, we round UP
- 4 or less, we round DOWN

EXAMPLE

Write 3.45759 to 2 decimal places (dp).

- The correct answer to this would be 3.46.
- For the this question, you need to round up.
- The second decimal digit is 5. So the number lies between 3.45 and 3.46
- So, we need to look at the NEXT number to determine the answer.
- The next digit is 7, so we have to round up our answer to 3.46

SIGNIFICANT FIGURES

Significant figures are similar to decimal places, but instead of focusing on the number after the decimal point, you need to focus on each number.

Write 3.45759 to 2 significant figures (sf).

- The correct answer to this would be 3.5.
- This is because the question is asking you to focus on the first 2 numbers. Since the second number is a 5, this means round up.

PERCENTAGES

Percentages are used to work out part of a number. For example, 25% of something is equivalent to ¼ or 0.25.

Percent ⟶ out of 100

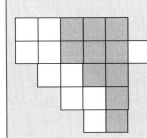

- To work out what percentage of this shape is shaded, you first need to work out the total number of squares.

Total number of squares = 20.

- Now work out the number of squares shaded.

Number of squares shaded = 10.

- There are 20 equal parts which means each square represents 5% (100 ÷ 20 = 5). So, 5% × 10 (shaded squares) = 50%

FIND X% OF Y

To express a number (x), as a percentage of another number (y) you will need to divide x by y and then multiply by 100.

35% of 300

Step 1 = 300 ÷ 100 = 3

Step 2 = 3 × 35 = 105.

Step 3 = 105 is 35% of 300.

Alternatively, you can convert the percentage into a decimal. So 35% becomes 0.35 × 300 = 105.

EXPRESSING X AS A PERCENTAGE OF Y

To express a number as a percentage of something else, you will need to divide x by y and then multiply by 100.

Write 30p as a percentage of £1.20

Step 1

Convert the pounds into pence. You need to work with the same units.

Step 2

Divide 30p by 120p.

$30 \div 120 = 0.25$

Step 3

Multiply this by 100.

$0.25 \times 100 = 25\%$

ROUNDING AND ESTIMATING

When to round up and when to round down

- When the units are LESS THAN 5, you will round down.

- When the units are MORE THAN 5, you will round up.

- If the unit IS 5, you will also round up!

Rounding to the nearest 10, 100, and 1,000

6453.4

- To the nearest whole number = 6453

- To the nearest 10 = 6450

- To the nearest 100 = 6500

- To the nearest 1,000 = 6000

Rounding to decimal places

STEP 1

Identify the number of decimal places you are trying to work out. For example, for 2 d.p. you will need to look at the second number **AFTER** the decimal point.

STEP 2

Then, look at the next digit to the right of this number. This is called the **DECIDER**.

- If it's 5 or higher, you will round up.
- If it's 4 or less, you will leave the number as it is.

MULTIPLES, FACTORS, AND PRIMES

Factors

Factors are numbers that can be divided **EXACTLY** into other numbers.

What are the factors of 60?

- 1 × 60 = 60
- 2 × 30 = 60
- 3 × 20 = 60
- 4 × 15 = 60
- 5 × 12 = 60
- 6 × 10 = 60

The factors of 60 are: 1, 2, 3, 4, 5 ,6, 10, 12, 15, 20, 30, 60.

Highest Common Factors (HCF)

Finding the 'highest common' factor of two or more numbers means finding the highest number that factorises into each of those numbers.

Find the highest common factor of 12 and 30.

Step 1

Work out the factors of 12.

- 1, 2, 3, 4, 6, 12

Step 2

Work out the factors of 30.

- 1, 2, 3, 5, 6, 10 15, 30

Step 3

Look out for the common factors. Which numbers occur in both sets?

- 1, 2, 3, 6

Step 4

So, the highest common factor is 6.

Prime Factors

The best way to work out the prime factors of a number is via a factor tree.

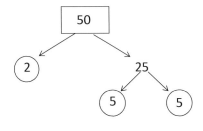

1. Find two factors to split the number (you can split the number any way you want)
2. Every time you find a prime number, circle it.
3. Keep going until you can no longer factorise.
4. The numbers you have circled are your prime factors.

So, the prime factors of 50 are 2 × 5 × 5.

Lowest Common Multiples (LCM)

Find the lowest common multiple of 2 and 5.

Step 1

Write out the first few multiples of 2.

2, 4, 6, 8, 10…

Step 2

Write out the first few multiples of 5.

5, 10, 15, 20, 25…

Step 3

Find the lowest multiple that both 2 and 5 have in common.

Step 4

The lowest common multiple for 2 and 5 is 10. (There is no smaller number that is a multiple of 2 and 5, therefore this is the correct answer).

SQUARE NUMBERS

To square a number, multiply the number by itself.

Squaring is usually represented by this symbol: ^{2}.

This is known as 'raising a number to the power of 2'.

2 x 2 = 4   *3 x 3 = 9*   *5 x 5 = 25*

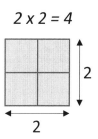

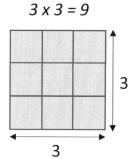

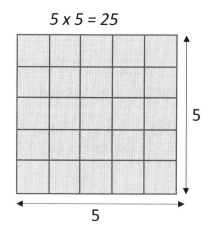

- $1^2 = 1 \times 1 = 1$
- $2^2 = 2 \times 2 = 4$
- $3^2 = 3 \times 3 = 9$
- $4^2 = 4 \times 4 = 16$

- $5^2 = 5 \times 5 = 25$
- $6^2 = 6 \times 6 = 36$
- $7^2 = 7 \times 7 = 49$
- $8^2 = 8 \times 8 = 64$

The number you have after doing the multiplication is called the **SQUARE NUMBER**.

SQUARE ROOTS

The square root of a number is a number that can be multiplied by itself, in order to give the original number.

1 2 9 16 25 36 49 64 81 100

HOW TO WORK OUT THE SQUARE ROOT:

Let's take the square number 49.

To work out the square root of that number, you are basically trying to find what number was multiplied by itself in order to reach that number.

The square root of 49 is 7.

SQUARE ROOT SYMBOL

 **25**

The square root of 25 is 5. (5 × 5 = 25)

CUBE NUMBERS

To cube a number, multiply it by itself three times. This is great for working out the VOLUME of 3D shapes!

Cubing is usually represented by this symbol: ^{3}.

This is known as 'raising a number to the power of 3'.

1 x 1 x 1 = 1   *2 x 2 x 2 = 8*   *3 x 3 x 3 = 27*

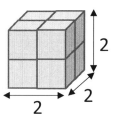

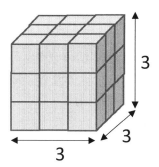

- $1^3 = 1 \times 1 \times 1 = 1$
- $2^3 = 2 \times 2 \times 2 = 8$
- $3^3 = 3 \times 3 \times 3 = 27$
- $4^3 = 4 \times 4 \times 4 = 64$
- $5^3 = 5 \times 5 \times 5 = 125$
- $6^3 = 6 \times 6 \times 6 = 216$
- $7^3 = 7 \times 7 \times 7 = 343$
- $8^3 = 8 \times 8 \times 8 = 512$

The number you have after doing the multiplication is called the **CUBE NUMBER**. The **CUBE ROOT** is the number that is multiplied to give you the cube number.

FRACTIONS, DECIMALS, AND PERCENTAGES

Understanding fractions

A fraction is **PART** of a whole number.

A **FRACTION** is made up of 2 numbers.

$\frac{2}{5}$ ⟶ The top number is called the NUMERATOR.
⟶ The bottom number is called the DENOMINATOR.

THE NUMERATOR

The numerator number tells you how many 'bits' we are <u>trying to work out</u>.

THE DENOMINATOR

The denominator number tells you how many equal parts there are '<u>altogether</u>'.

Simplifying fractions

$$\overset{\div 4}{\overset{\frown}{\underset{\underset{\div 4}{\smile}}{\frac{60}{80}}}} = \overset{\div 5}{\overset{\frown}{\underset{\underset{\div 5}{\smile}}{\frac{15}{20}}}} = \frac{3}{4} \qquad\qquad \overset{\div 9}{\overset{\frown}{\underset{\underset{\div 9}{\smile}}{\frac{27}{135}}}} = \overset{\div 3}{\overset{\frown}{\underset{\underset{\div 3}{\smile}}{\frac{3}{15}}}} = \frac{1}{5}$$

Adding and subtracting fractions

CROSSBOW METHOD ADDING

$$\frac{3}{4} + \frac{2}{5} = \frac{15 + 8}{20} = \frac{23}{20} = 1\frac{3}{20}$$

Draw two diagonal lines through both of the fractions as shown. (This forms the **CROSS** which looks like a multiplication sign).

It tells you to multiply the 3 by 5 = 15
It tells you to multiply the 4 by 2 = 8.

15 + 8 = 23

Then draw your **BOW** (from the bottom number of the first fraction to the bottom number of the second fraction).

Again, multiply these two numbers: 4 × 5 = 20

Done! (Some fractions will be able to be simplified, as shown in the above example).

CROSSBOW METHOD SUBTRACTING

$$\frac{4}{7} - \frac{1}{3} = \frac{12 - 7}{21} = \frac{5}{21}$$

Remember to keep the numbers in the correct order! 12 (4 × 3) must go before 7 (7 × 1).

Draw two diagonal lines through both of the fractions as shown. (This forms the **CROSS** which looks like a multiplication sign).

It tells you to multiply the 4 by 3 = 12
It tells you to multiply the 7 by 1 = 7.
12 − 7 = 5

Then draw your **BOW** (from the bottom number of the first fraction to the bottom number of the second fraction).

Again, multiply these two numbers: 7 × 3 = 21

Multiplying and dividing fractions

ARROW METHOD MULTIPLYING

$$\frac{5}{9} \times \frac{3}{5} = \frac{15}{45} = \frac{3}{9} = \frac{1}{3}$$

Draw an arrow through the two top numbers and multiply.
5 × 3 = 15

Draw an arrow through the two bottom numbers.
9 × 5 = 45

Done! (Some fractions will be able to be simplified, as shown in the above example).

ARROW METHOD DIVIDING

$$\frac{4}{7} \div \frac{3}{4} = \frac{4}{7} \times \frac{4}{3} = \frac{16}{21}$$

This is actually quite simple. Turn the second fraction upside down. Change the division sign to a multiplication sign, and then use the **SAME** method as if you were multiplying.

You will get the answer correct every time!

Key thing to remember:

When you are dividing two fractions, don't forget to turn the second fraction **UPSIDE DOWN** before you multiply the numbers.

METRIC AND IMPERIAL UNITS

METRIC and IMPERIAL units are types of measurements.

METRIC UNITS	IMPERIAL UNITS
LENGTH mm, cm, m, km	**LENGTH** inches, yards, feet, miles
AREA mm², cm², m², km²	**AREA** square inches, square feet, square miles
VOLUME mm³, cm³, m³, ml, litres	**VOLUME** pints, cubic inches, cubic feet, gallons
MASS (WEIGHT) g, kg, tonnes	**MASS (WEIGHT)** ounces, pounds, stones, tons
SPEED km/h, m/s	**SPEED** mph

METRIC CONVERSIONS

- 1 cm = 10 mm
- 1 m = 100 cm
- 1 km = 1000 m
- 1 kg = 1000 g
- 1 tonne = 1000 kg
- 1 litre = 1000 ml
- 1 litre = 1000 cm³
- 1 cm³ = 1 ml

Learn these off by heart!

IMPERIAL CONVERSIONS

- 1 foot = 12 inches
- 1 yard = 3 feet
- 1 gallon = 8 pints
- 1 stone = 14 pounds
- 1 pound = 16 ounces

Learn these off by heart!

CONVERSIONS!

You should try to learn as many of these as you can:

The symbol '≈' means 'approximately' or 'nearly equal to'

METRIC–IMPERIAL

- 1 inch ≈ 2.54 cm
- 1 kg ≈ 2.2 pounds
- 1 litre ≈ 1.75 pints
- 1 mile ≈ 1.6 km

IMPERIAL–METRIC

- 1 foot ≈ 30 cm
- 1 gallon ≈ 4.5 litres

SPEED, DISTANCE, AND TIME

You need to know the relationship between speed, distance and time.

Sometimes, you will be required to work out one of the above, based on the information you are given. To do this, there is a simple formula that you **MUST** remember:

The below triangle shows the relationship between speed, distance and time.

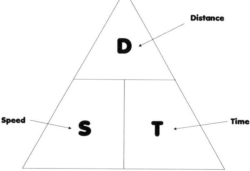

HOW TO WORK OUT SPEED

To work out the average speed, place your thumb over the speed variable ('S'), and then do the calculation.

- Speed = Distance ÷ Time

HOW TO WORK OUT DISTANCE

To work out the distance travelled, place your thumb over the distance variable ('D'), and then work out the equation.

- Distance = Speed × Time

HOW TO WORK OUT TIME

To work out the time taken, place your thumb over the time variable ('T'), and then work out the equation.

- Time = Distance ÷ Speed

SCALE FACTOR OF ENLARGEMENTS

Proportions can also be used to compare lengths of shapes.

To find the scale factor of an enlargement, divide a length on the enlarged shape by a corresponding length on the original shape.

You need to learn the relationship between the different scale factors for length, area, and volume.

LENGTH	AREA	VOLUME
×2	×4	×8
×3	×9	×27

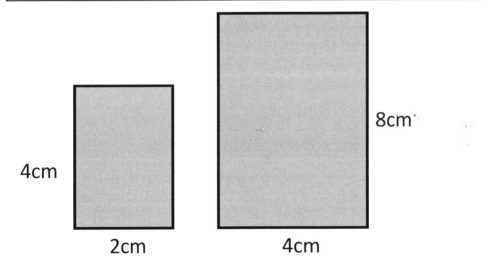

4cm

2cm

8cm

4cm

- To work out the scale factor:

8 ÷ 4 = 2cm

- The lengths on the larger rectangle are twice the size of the lengths on the smaller rectangle.

BEARINGS

When talking about directions, we often need to refer to something called bearings.

Bearings are used to give directions from point A to point B.

Bearings are often used in scale drawing questions. They are always measured from the North point, they are measured in a clockwise direction, and they are always written with three figures.

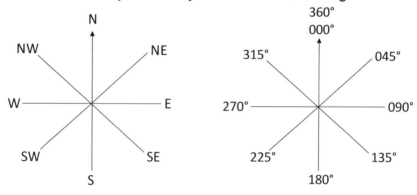

For example, to measure the bearing of A from B:

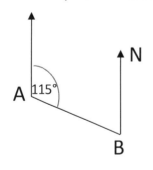

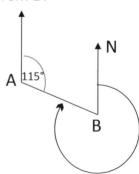

- Acute Angle $ABN = 180° - 115° = 65°$

- Reflect Angle ABN, which is the bearing of A from B, $360° - 65° = 295°$

- $= 295°$

PRESSURE / FORCE / AREA

Pressure is all about the amount of **force** that is being exerted per unit **area**.

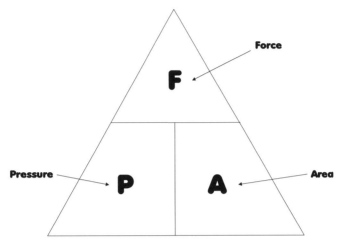

In GCSE Maths, the units of pressure are compound:

- Pounds per square inch;
- Kilograms per square metre;
- Grams per square centimetre etc.

EXAMPLE

The surface area of an object is 0.45 metres squared. A person has a mass of 65 kilograms. How much pressure, in kg/m², does the person exert on the object?

- The question is telling us: divide the number of kilograms by the number of metres squared.
- 65 ÷ 0.25 = 260
- So, the pressure is 260 kg/m².

TRIGONOMETRY

Each side of a triangle has a special name:
HYPOTENUSE, OPPOSITE and ADJACENT

Each one of the names above links two sides and an angle. Again, this only works with **RIGHT-ANGLED TRIANGLES.**

The hypotenuse = the longest side of the triangle.

The opposite = the opposite side to the angle being used (x)

The adjacent = is the other side next to the angle being used.

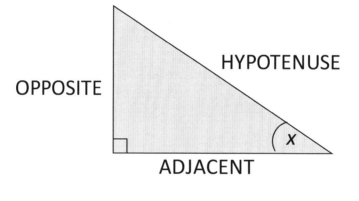

DON'T FORGET:
SOH   CAH   TOA

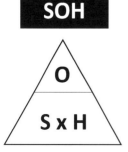 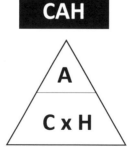 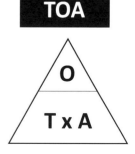

There are three formulas that you need to understand.

$$\text{Sin } x = \frac{Opposite}{Hypotenuse} \qquad \text{Cos } x = \frac{Adjacent}{Hypotenuse} \qquad \text{Tan } x = \frac{Opposite}{Adjacent}$$

Key things to remember:

- When you have a question on trigonometry, you should first look at which two sides are involved in the question (either given sides, or a side you are trying to find). (O,H   A,H   or   O,A)

- From that, you will be able to choose which formula you need to use to solve the question. (**SOH**,   **CAH**,   **TOA**)

- Then using the formula, use the triangles above to show you how to correctly use each formula.

- Cover up the thing you are trying to find, and do the calculation that is left.

EXAMPLE

Work out the length of the opposite side. Give your answer to 1 decimal place.

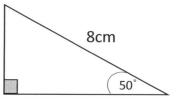

STEP 1

Label the sides.

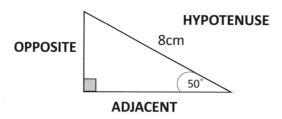

STEP 2

The opposite and the hypotenuse are involved, so the formula we will use is **SOH.**

STEP 3

We are trying to work out O, so cover it up and do the calculation:

$= \mathbf{s}\text{in } 50° × 8 = 6.12$

To 1 decimal place = 6.1cm

HOW TO TACKLE WORD PROBLEMS

Tackling word problems is relatively easy once you know the simple rule, and that rule is this: break up the problem, and pick out all of the key information you need in order to solve the maths problem.

EXAMPLE

A school has organised a school trip to London to see a show. In total there are 45 children and 9 adults attending. Work out the ratio of children to adults attending the trip. Give your answer in its simplest form.

As you can see, the above example is full of lots of information. Let's make this easier to understand:

~~A school has organised a school trip to London to see a show. In total there are~~ 45 children and 9 adults ~~attending.~~ Work out the ratio of children to adults ~~attending the trip. Give your answer in its~~ simplest form.

Now we are left with the following information:

- 45 children
- 9 adults
- Work out the ratio (in its simplest form).
- = 45 : 9   5 : 1

NUMBERS

Day 1

INDICES

Indices are also known as a **power**.

Here is a number written in index form:

$$5^6$$

This is a short way of writing $5 \times 5 \times 5 \times 5 \times 5 \times 5$.

The power or index number shows how many times a number is multiplied by itself.

This can be used in algebra too:

$$a^4$$

This is a short way of writing $a \times a \times a \times a$.

The Laws of Indices

$a^n \times a^m = a^{n+m}$	$a^n \div a^m = a^{n-m}$	$(a^n)^m = a^{n \times m}$	$a^0 = 1$
$a^1 = a$	$a^{-n} = \dfrac{1}{a^n}$	$a^{\frac{1}{m}} = (\sqrt[m]{a})$	$a^{\frac{n}{m}} = (\sqrt[m]{a})^n$

DAY 1 ➡ **Numbers**

Activity I

Q1. Simplify the following calculations:

a) $8^6 \times 8^{10}$

b) $(x^6)^4$

c) $9^{11} \div 9^7$

d) $(8^4 \times 8^{12}) \div 8^2$

STANDARD FORM

Standard form is a great way to write really **LARGE** or really **SMALL** numbers.

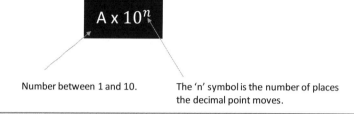

$$A \times 10^n$$

Number between 1 and 10.   The 'n' symbol is the number of places the decimal point moves.

Express 346,000 in standard form.

STEP 1

Move the decimal point so that the first number is between 1 and 10.

- 3.46 ($1 \leq A < 10$)

STEP 2

Count how many places the decimal point has moved = 5.

This gives us 10^5

STEP 3

So we have 3.46×10^5

- If you are dealing with a large number, n will be **POSITIVE**.
- If you are dealing with a small number, n will be **NEGATIVE**.
- If you are asked to work out a calculation which contains standard form, you will need to first work out the number, and then do the calculation.
- If you are asked to write out numbers from smallest to biggest, you will need to make sure all of the numbers are written in standard form. Next you will group the numbers with the same **POWER**, and order them accordingly. Lastly, arrange the groups of numbers based on the front number.

DAY 1 ➡   **Numbers**

Activity 2

Q1. Change this number from its standard index form to its actual number.

$$1.43 \times 10^3$$

Q2. Change this number from its standard index form to its actual number.

$$1.6 \times 10^3$$

Q3. Arrange these numbers in order from smallest to biggest.

3.35×10^5 6.34×10^{-3} 5530   0.00035

FINANCES

Finances are important for not only your exams, but for the real world, too!

SALARY

When you go to work, you will be paid a salary. A salary is the amount of money you earn, usually over a year's time.

For example:

If you earned a salary of £30,000 per year, your monthly pay would be 30,000 ÷ 12 = £2,500. This is the **gross pay**.

The gross pay is the amount of money **BEFORE** deductions.

The net pay is what's left **AFTER** deductions are made.

Deductions will include tax and National Insurance. It could also include any Pension Scheme Contribution.

Two words that you should bear in mind are **INCREASE** and **DECREASE**.

- An increase is the addition of money i.e. making a profit.
- A decrease is a reduction in money i.e. making a loss.

PERCENTAGE INCREASE AND PERCENTAGE DECREASE

To work out the percentage increase of a set of data, you need to remember this formula:

PERCENT INCREASE % = DIFFERENCE ÷ ORIGINAL NUMBER × 100

To work out the percentage decrease of a set of data, you need to remember this formula:

PERCENT DECREASE % = DIFFERENCE ÷ ORIGINAL NUMBER × 100

VAT

VAT (Value Added Tax) is paid to the government. VAT is added to items that you buy, except for things that are deemed essential, such as food.

As it currently stands, the VAT is set at 20%.

For example:

A car costs £8,000, without tax. Including tax, what is the total cost of the car?

- $120\% \times 8{,}000 = \dfrac{120}{100} \times 8{,}000 = \dfrac{120 \times 8{,}000}{100} = £9{,}600$

Activity 3

1. Michael is saving money to buy his first house. Currently, Michael has £3,800 in his bank account. His bank account pays 5% interest each year. How much money will Michael have after the first year?

2. In April, John earned £2,870. On his payslip, it shows that John was taxed £574. What percentage rate of tax did John pay?

3. Michael wants to buy a new house. The house he is looking at is currently £320,000. The house market is set to drop its prices in the next month. Michael has a limit of £102,400. By what percentage does the house market need to drop its price in order for Michael to be able to afford the house?

4. The following table shows the prices of a travel agents holiday prices for booking holidays for next year.

HOLIDAY PRICES				
Types of Holiday Deals	Turkey	Mexico	America	Spain
All inclusive	£276pp	£720pp	£880pp	£320pp
Half board	£220pp	£640pp	£795pp	£275pp
Self-Catering	£180pp	£550pp	£620pp	£235pp

How much would it cost for a family of five to book a holiday, all inclusive, to America? They have a 20% discount voucher on the total price.

SURDS

A surd is an expression that uses a root symbol, for example a square root($\sqrt{}$) or cubed root($^3\sqrt{}$), to write an irrational number.

Surds are used for accuracy as irrational numbers cannot be written precisely as they do not recur or terminate.

EXAMPLE $\sqrt{16} = 4$ is NOT a surd

$\sqrt{8} = 2.828427...$ IS a surd

For GCSE Maths, you need to be able to simplify surds.

$$\sqrt{ab} = \sqrt{a} \times \sqrt{b}$$

$$\sqrt{24} = \sqrt{4} \times \sqrt{6}$$

$$\sqrt{24} = 2\sqrt{6}$$

$$\sqrt{a} \times \sqrt{a} = a$$

$$\sqrt{15} \times \sqrt{5} = \sqrt{75}$$

$$\sqrt{75} = \sqrt{25} \times \sqrt{3}$$

$$\sqrt{75} = 5\sqrt{3}$$

$$\frac{\sqrt{a}}{\sqrt{b}} = \sqrt{\frac{a}{b}} = \sqrt{a \div b}$$

$$\frac{\sqrt{24}}{\sqrt{12}} = \sqrt{\frac{24}{12}} = \sqrt{24 \div 12} = \sqrt{2}$$

DAY 1 ➡   **Numbers**

Activity 4

1) Simplify:

$$\sqrt{3} \times \sqrt{12}$$

2) Simplify:

$$\sqrt{\frac{16}{8}}$$

3) Simplify:

$$2\sqrt{5} \times 3\sqrt{5}$$

4) Simplify:

$$\sqrt{12 \div 8}$$

ANSWERS TO CHAPTER I

INDICES

1a) 8^{16}

- When you multiply, you will need to ADD the powers.

1b)x^{24}

- When you are raising one power to another, you will need to MULTIPLY the two powers.

1c) 9^4

- When you divide, you will need to SUBTRACT the two powers.

1d)8^{14}

- $(8^{16}) \div 8^2 = 8^{14}$

STANDARD FORM

Q1.

1,430

Q2.

1,600

Q3.

0.00035 6.34×10^{-3} 5,530 3.35×10^5

- 3.5×10^{-4} = 0.00035
- 6.34×10^{-3} = 0.00634
- 5.53×10^3 = 5,530
- 3.35×10^5 = 335,000

FINANCES

Q1. £3,990

- $3,800 \div 100 = 38$
- $38 \times 105 = 3,990$

Q2. 20%

- $574 \div 2,870 = 0.2$
- $0.2 \times 100 = 20\%$

Q3. 68%

- $320,000 - 102,400 = 217,600$
- $217,600 \div 320,000 = 0.68$
- $0.68 \times 100 = 68\%$

Q4. £3,520

- $5 \times 880 = £4,400$
- $4,400 \div 100 = 44$
- $44 \times 80 = 3,520$

SURDS

Q1.

$\sqrt{3} \times \sqrt{12}$

$\sqrt{3} \times \sqrt{12} = \sqrt{3 \times 12}$

$\sqrt{3 \times 12} = \sqrt{36}$

$\sqrt{36} = 6$

Q2.

$\sqrt{\dfrac{16}{8}} = \sqrt{16 \div 8}$

$\sqrt{16 \div 8} = \sqrt{2}$

Q3.

$2\sqrt{5} \times 3\sqrt{5} = 6\sqrt{25}$

$6\sqrt{25} = 6 \times 5$

$6 \times 5 = 30$

Q4.

$\sqrt{12 \div 8} = \sqrt{\dfrac{12}{8}}$

$\sqrt{\dfrac{12}{8}} = \sqrt{\dfrac{3}{2}}$

Day 1 Checklist

You have now completed your Day 1 revision.

How confident are you feeling?

Below we have included a checklist that you can tick off to make sure that you have learnt everything regarding this chapter.

I have read and understood the examples for tackling different number calculations.

I have tackled all of the questions in this section.

I have read and understood the answers in this section.

I feel confident in Numbers questions.

RATIO, PROPORTION, AND RATES OF CHANGE

Day 2

RATIO

Ratios are a way of showing how things are shared.

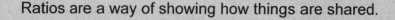

As you can see, we have 8 squares.

There are 4 white squares, and 4 black squares.

If we wanted to write this as a ratio we would write it as follows:

4 : 4

If you had a question asking what ratio of black squares there are to white squares, you would need to write the number of black squares first.

Work out the ratio of shaded squares to white squares.

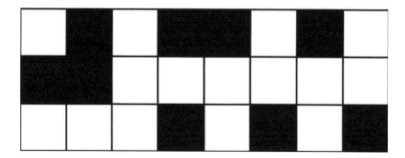

Step 1

Add up the total number of squares.

- There are 24 squares in total.

> Pay attention to what order you put the numbers in. The numbers must represent each part of the question.

Step 2

Next, work out the number of shaded squares, and the number of white squares.

- There are 9 shaded squares and 15 white squares.

Therefore, the ratio of shaded squares to white squares is 9 : 15.

This can be simplified to 3 : 5.

The process of simplifying is quite easy. All you have to do is find a number that both values of the ratio can be divided by.

The ratio will be in its simplest form, when there are no numbers that can be divided into both values of the ratio.

EXAMPLE

Simplify 40 : 60. Write your answer in its simplest form.

Step 1

Both '40' and '60' can be divided by 10.

*   If you divide both numbers by 10, you get the ratio: 4 : 6

Step 2

Both '4' and '6' can be divided by 2.

*   If you divide both numbers by 2, you would get the ratio: 2 : 3

Step 3

No other numbers can be divided equally into 2 and 3, so 2 : 3 is the simplest form of 40 : 60.

See how the ratios 40 : 60, 4 : 6 and 2 : 3 are all equivalent ratios = they all mean the same thing!

The same principles apply for splitting a number into more than 2 parts.

When you're working with ratios, sometimes you might be given the ratio, and then given a size of an actual part.

Your job is to work out the other size, based on the ratio given.

EXAMPLE

Jason and Matthew each have elastic bands in the ratio of 6 : 4.

If Jason has 42 elastic bands, how many elastic bands does Matthew have?

Step 1

First of all, we need to work out what Jason's share of the ratio (6) is multiplied by to make 42.

$$6 : 4$$

$$42 : ?$$

Step 2

You can multiply the 6 by 7 to give you 42.

Step 3

That means we must multiply the other side of the ratio by 7 to work out how many elastic bands Matthew has.

$$x7 \left(\begin{array}{c} 6 : 4 \\ 42 : 28 \end{array} \right) x7$$

REMEMBER

Whatever you do to one part of the ratio, has to be done to the other part of the ratio!

Activity 1

Q1. Below there are 10 cards. Each card has a ratio. Match the equivalent boxes from the top row to its simplest ratio in the bottom row.

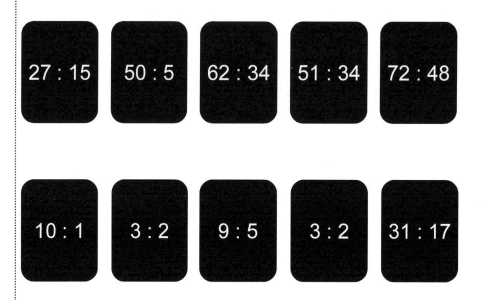

Q2. A school has organised a school trip to London to see a show.

In total there are 45 children and 9 adults attending.

Work out the ratio of children to adults attending the trip. Give your answer in its simplest form.

PROPORTION

Proportional division is very simple to understand.

This is where you will be given a total, and you have to split that total into proportions given by a ratio.

There are 3 steps that you need to follow in order to work out proportional division correctly.

STEP 1

Add up the two parts of the ratio.

STEP 2

Take the total you wish to split up and divide it by the sum of the ratio parts you worked out in step 1.

STEP 3

Multiply your answer from step 2 by the numbers on each side of the ratio to get the two amounts the total is split into."

EXAMPLE

Tim and Tom are going to share £800 in the ratio of 13 : 7. How much will Tim's share be?

Step 1

Add up the ratios = 13 + 7 = 20

Step 2

Divide 800 by 20 = 800 ÷ 20 = 40

Step 3

Multiply the 40 by Tim's share (which is 13) = 40 × 13 = £520

Activity 2

Q1. William has made a fruit punch. He uses three ingredients: apple juice, orange juice and cranberry juice.

He needs to make a total of 750 ml of fruit punch.

If his recipe for his fruit juice is in the ratio of 11 : 8 : 6, work out how much of each ingredient he will need to make enough fruit punch.

Q2. 4 decorators can decorate 12 rooms in one day. How many rooms could be decorated if there were 16 decorators?

Q3. Harrison, Katie and Ryan all work in a restaurant during their summer holidays.

In total, they earn £780 in tips in just 6 weeks.

They decide to split the money in the ratio of the number of hours each person worked. The ratio they split these tips into is 12 : 8 : 20.

Calculate how much each person will receive in tips.

DIRECT PROPORTION

Direct proportion refers to the relationship between two changing variables.

If one quantity increases in the same proportion as another quantity, this is called direct proportion.

<u>For example:</u>

10 mm = 1 cm.

Direct proportion is often used to calculate the cost of petrol or exchange rates between different currencies.

The symbol for DIRECT PROPORTION is:

For example, the cost of a bag of potatoes is directly proportional to the weight of the potatoes.

If y is directly proportional to x:

- If $y = kx$, the graph y against x is going to be a straight line.

- The constant of the proportionality will determine the line's gradient.

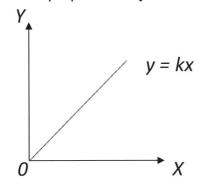

DAY 2 → Ratio, Proportion, and Rates of Change

Activity 3

Q1. If a is proportional to b and $a = 6$ when $b = 9$, find the value of k (the constant of proportionality) and the value of a when $b = 3$.

Q2. a is directly proportional to x. When $x = 2$, $a = 6$. What is the constant of proportionality and what is the value of x when $a = 40$?

INVERSE PROPORTION

Indirect proportion is when one quantity increases as the other decreases, or vice versa.

If y is inversely proportional to x, then you should write the following:

- $y \propto {}^{1}/x$ or $y = {}^{k}/x$

For example:

If the number of workers on a task doubles, then the time to complete the task halves. If the number of workers triples then the time would be one third of its previous value.

The symbol for INVERSE PROPORTION is:

$$b \propto \frac{1}{m}$$

Activity 4

Q1. a is inversely proportional to b^2. Given that $a = 4.5$ when $b = 15$. Find an equation for a in terms of b.

Q2. y is inversely proportional to x. When $x = 4$, $y = 12$.

Calculate y when $x = 2$.

ANSWERS TO DAY 2

RATIO

ACTIVITY 1

Q1.

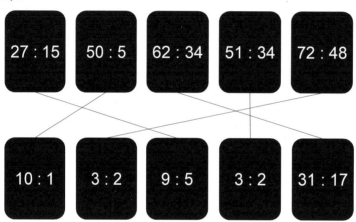

Q2.

5 : 1

- The ratio of children to adults is 45 : 9.
- Both 45 and 9 are divisible by 9.
- In its simplest form the ratio is 5 : 1.
- (There are 5 students to every 1 adult).

PROPORTION

ACTIVITY 2

Q1.

330 ml apple   240 ml orange   180 ml cranberry

- 11 + 8 + 6 = 25
- 750 ÷ 25 = 30
- 30 × 11 = 330 apple juice
- 30 × 8 = 240 orange juice
- 30 × 6 = 180 cranberry juice

Q2.

48

- 12 ÷ 4 = 3
- 3 × 16 = 48

Q3.

Harrison = £234

Katie = £156

Ryan = £390

- 12 : 8 : 20 = 12 + 8 + 20 = 40
- £780 ÷ 40 = 19.5
- 19.5 × 12 = £234 (Harrison)

- 19.5 × 8 = £156 (Katie)
- 19.5 × 20 = £390 (Ryan)

DIRECT PROPORTION

ACTIVITY 3

Q1.

2

- $6 = k \times 9$
- $\frac{6}{9} = k$
- Replace k with value just found:
- $a = \frac{6}{9}b$
- If $b = 3$: $a = \frac{6}{9} \times 3 = 2$

Q2.

$a = 4x$

- $a = kx$
- $6 = 2k$
- $k = 3$
- $a = 3x$
- Constant of probability = 3
- $40 = 3x$
- $x = \dfrac{40}{3}$

INDIRECT PROPORTION

ACTIVITY 4

Q1.

$$a = \frac{1012.5}{b^2}$$

Q2.

$y = 24$

- $y = k/x$

- $12 = k/_4$

- $k = 48$

- $y = {}^{48}/_2$

- $y = 24$

Day 2 Checklist

You have now completed your Day 2 revision.

How confident are you feeling?

Below we have included a checklist that you can tick off to make sure that you have learnt everything regarding this chapter.

I have read and understood the examples for tackling Ratio, Proportion, and Rates of Change questions.

I have tackled all of the questions in this section.

I have read and understood the answers in this section.

I feel confident in Ratio, Proportion, and Rates of Change questions.

GEOMETRY AND MEASUREMENTS

Day 3

ANGLES

An angle is a way of measuring a turn. The size of the angle will determine the ANGLE NAME.

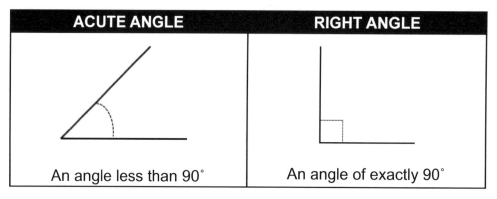

ACUTE ANGLE	RIGHT ANGLE
An angle less than 90°	An angle of exactly 90°

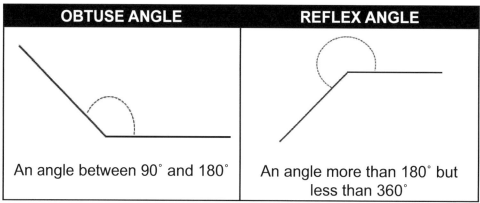

OBTUSE ANGLE	REFLEX ANGLE
An angle between 90° and 180°	An angle more than 180° but less than 360°

ANGLES IN A TRIANGLE

The angles in a triangle will **ALWAYS** add up to 180°.

DAY 3 ➡ **Geometry and Measures**

EQUILATERAL TRIANGLE	ISOSCELES TRIANGLE
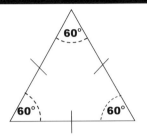	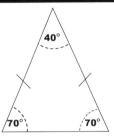
All angles are equal. Each angle would be 60˚.	Two angles are of equal size.

SCALENE TRIANGLE	RIGHT-ANGLED TRIANGLE
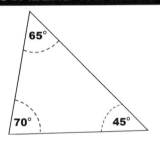	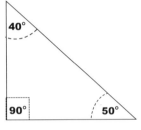
None of the angles are the same size.	One of the angles will be 90˚.

ANGLES IN A QUADRILATERAL

The angles in a quadrilateral will **ALWAYS** add up to 360˚.

QUADRILATERAL	PARALLELOGRAM
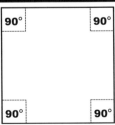	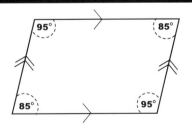
A square contains four 90˚ angles, so does a rectangle.	A parallelogram contains two pairs of equal angles, which add up to 360˚.

DAY 3 ➡ **Geometry and Measures**

ANGLES OF STRAIGHT LINES AND CIRCLES

The angles on a straight line will **ALWAYS** add up to 180°.

The angles around a point will **ALWAYS** add up to 360°.

STRAIGHT LINE	CIRCLE
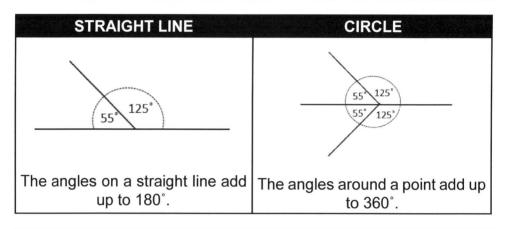	
The angles on a straight line add up to 180°.	The angles around a point add up to 360°.

ANGLE NOTATIONS

Sometimes, you may be asked to talk about a particular angle.

In this instance, the best way to do this is via angle notation. Angle notation uses three letters to describe which angle you are talking about.

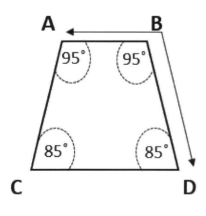

- If you are talking about angle B, you could describe the angle as **ABD** = 95°.

- If you are talking about angle C, you could describe the angle as **ACD** = 85°.

The middle letter in the notation is the actual angle, the other letters tell you which two lines join to make this angle.

LINES

PARALLEL LINES

Parallel lines are lines which are going in the exact same direction.

These lines NEVER touch, and are ALWAYS the same distance away from each other.

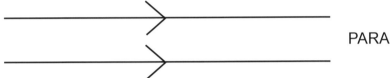

PARALLEL LINES

ALTERNATE 'Z' LINES

Alternate (Z) angles are always the same size.

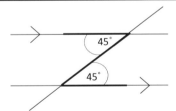

CORRESPONDING 'F' LINES

Corresponding (F) angles are always the same size.

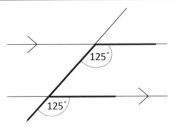

ALLIED 'C' OR 'U' LINES

ALLIED angles will add up to 180°.

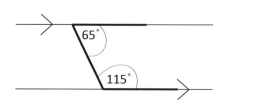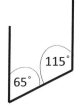

VERTICALLY OPPOSITE

VERTICALLY OPPOSITE angles are equal to one another.

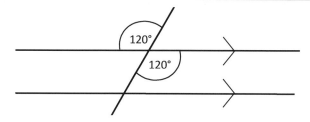

Activity I

Q1.

Work out the angle z.

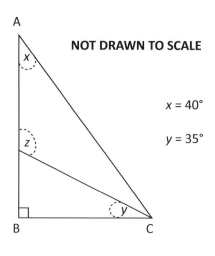

A

NOT DRAWN TO SCALE

$x = 40°$

$y = 35°$

B C

Q2.

Work out the value of x.

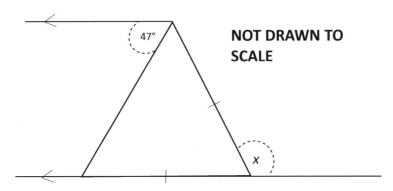

47°

NOT DRAWN TO SCALE

x

Q3.

Work out the missing angles.

NOT DRAWN TO SCALE

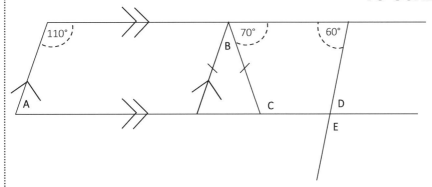

110°

70°

60°

A

B

C

D

E

A =

B =

C =

D =

E =

MIDPOINT OF A LINE

The midpoint of a line is easy to find, especially if you draw out a diagram.

EXAMPLE

What is the midpoint of the line between (2, 7) and (4, 1)?

- The number between '2' and '4' is '3'. This is the middle number.

- The number between '7' and '1' is '4'. This is the middle number.

- So the midpoint would be (3, 4).

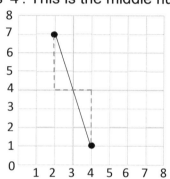

GRADIENT OF A LINE

To find the gradient of a line:

- Choose two points on the line (any two points).

- Draw a right-angled triangle.

- Use the scale to find the triangle's height and width.

- Vertical length ÷ horizontal length = gradient

- $4 ÷ 8 = -½$

This gradient is negative.

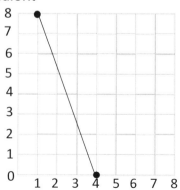

DAY 3 ➡ **Geometry and Measures**

ROTATIONAL SYMMETRY

The 'order of rotational symmetry' refers to the number of different positions the shape has which look identical.

| Rotational symmetry order 1 | Rotational symmetry order 2 | Rotational symmetry order 3 | Rotational symmetry order 4 |

Activity 2

Q1.

How many lines of symmetry does this shape have?

Q2.

Which lines are perpendicular?

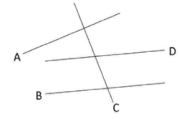

2D SHAPES

2D shapes are shapes that only have two dimensions – length and width.

When it comes to 2D shapes, there are two types you need to know about:

* Regular polygons;

* Irregular polygons.

REGULAR POLYGONS

EQUILATERAL TRIANGLE	NO. OF SIDES	LINES OF SYMMETRY	ROTATIONAL SYMMETRY
	• 3 sides	• 3 lines of symmetry	• Rotational symmetry of order 3

SQUARE	NO. OF SIDES	LINES OF SYMMETRY	ROTATIONAL SYMMETRY
	• 4 sides	• 4 lines of symmetry	• Rotational symmetry of order 4

PENTAGON	NO. OF SIDES	LINES OF SYMMETRY	ROTATIONAL SYMMETRY
	• 5 sides	• 5 lines of symmetry	• Rotational symmetry of order 5

HEXAGON	NO. OF SIDES	LINES OF SYMMETRY	ROTATIONAL SYMMETRY
	• 6 sides	• 6 lines of symmetry	• Rotational symmetry of order 6

HEPTAGON	NO. OF SIDES	LINES OF SYMMETRY	ROTATIONAL SYMMETRY
	• 7 sides	• 7 lines of symmetry	• Rotational symmetry of order 7

OCTAGON	NO. OF SIDES	LINES OF SYMMETRY	ROTATIONAL SYMMETRY
	• 8 sides	• 8 lines of symmetry	• Rotational symmetry of order 8

All of these examples are shapes of 'regular' polygons.

DAY 3 ➡ **Geometry and Measures**

CONGRUENT SHAPES

Congruent shapes are shapes that are EXACTLY the same shape and size.

This includes shapes that are rotations or reflections.

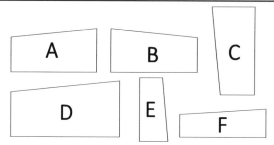

A, B, and C are congruent. B is a reflection of A and C is a rotation of A.

D, E, and F are all different sizes and therefore cannot be congruent.

The symbol ≡ means 'is congruent to'.

CONGRUENT TRIANGLES

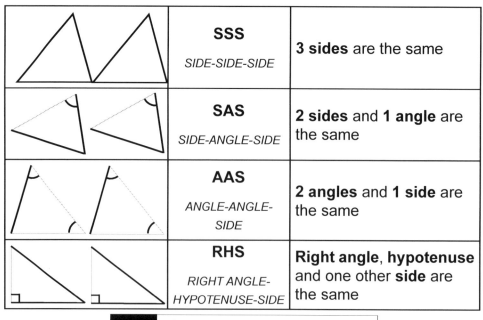	**SSS** *SIDE-SIDE-SIDE*	**3 sides** are the same
	SAS *SIDE-ANGLE-SIDE*	**2 sides** and **1 angle** are the same
	AAS *ANGLE-ANGLE-SIDE*	**2 angles** and **1 side** are the same
	RHS *RIGHT ANGLE-HYPOTENUSE-SIDE*	**Right angle, hypotenuse** and one other **side** are the same

IRREGULAR POLYGONS

An irregular polygon is a shape which has different size lengths.

Let's go through some of the properties of some irregular polygon shapes.

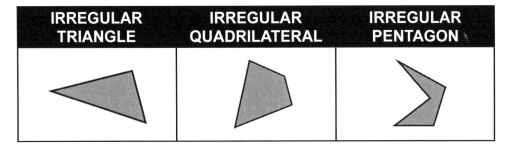

IRREGULAR TRIANGLE	IRREGULAR QUADRILATERAL	IRREGULAR PENTAGON
IRREGULAR HEXAGON	IRREGULAR HEPTAGON	IRREGULAR OCTAGON

A polygon is irregular if at least 2 of its sides or angles are different.

Activity 3

Q1.

Fill in the table.

Name of shape	No. of sides	Lines of symmetry
Square		
	6	
		8
Regular Heptagon		

Q2.

Work out how many lines of symmetry the following shapes have:

- Regular Nonagon

- Equilateral Triangle

- Regular Octagon

Q3.

Circle the congruent shapes.

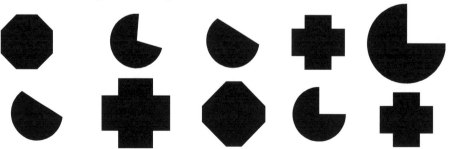

3D SHAPES

3D shapes are SOLID shapes.

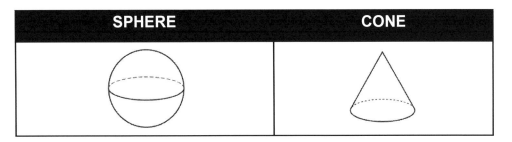

SPHERE	CONE

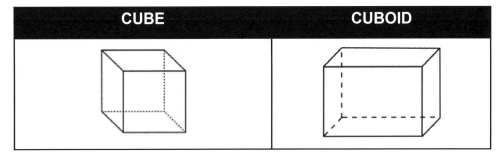

CUBE	CUBOID

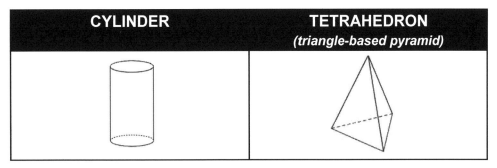

CYLINDER	TETRAHEDRON *(triangle-based pyramid)*

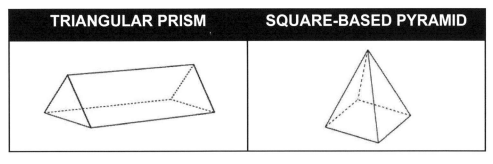

TRIANGULAR PRISM	SQUARE-BASED PYRAMID

DAY 3 → **Geometry and Measures**

When it comes to 3D shapes, there are also some other **KEY WORDS** that you need to be aware of:

- Face;
- Vertex;
- Edge.

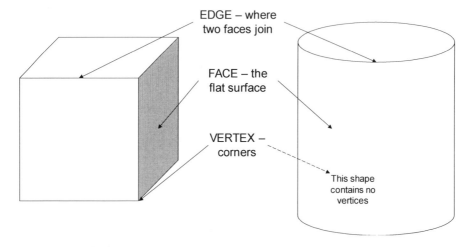

EDGE – where two faces join

FACE – the flat surface

VERTEX – corners

This shape contains no vertices

NETS OF 3D SHAPES

The **NET** of a shape is what the shape would look like if it was opened out flat.

There is often more than one net for each solid shape.

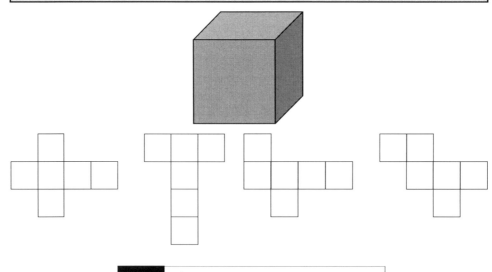

DAY 3 ➡ **Geometry and Measures**

CUBOID	CUBOID NET

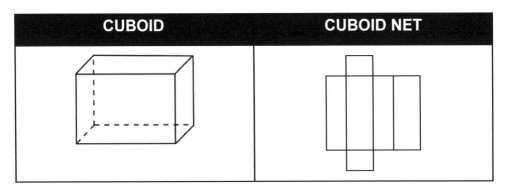

TETRAHEDRON	TETRAHEDRON NET

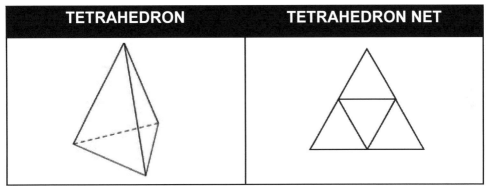

SQUARE-BASED PYRAMID	SQUARE-BASED PYRAMID NET

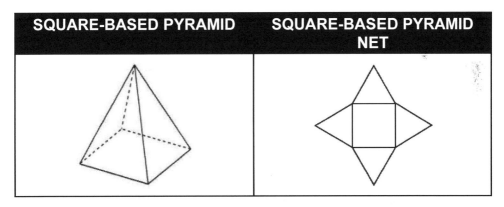

TRIANGULAR PRISM	TRIANGULAR PRISM NET

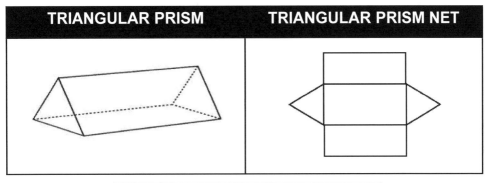

DAY 3 → **Geometry and Measures**

VOLUME OF 3D SHAPES

The **VOLUME** of a shape is the space inside it! The surface area of a 3D shape is the total area of ALL the faces.

VOLUME OF A CUBE/CUBOID	VOLUME OF A PRISM
length (l) × width (w) × height (h)	area of the cross section × length (l)

VOLUME OF A CYLINDER	VOLUME OF A PYRAMID
$\pi\, r^2\, h$ Pi × radius^2 × height (h)	$^1/_3$ × area of base × perpendicular height

VOLUME OF A CONE	VOLUME OF A SPHERE
$\frac{1}{3}\,\pi\, r^2\, h$	$\frac{4}{3}\,\pi\, r^3$

SURFACE AREA OF 3D SHAPES

The **SURFACE AREA** of a shape is the sum of the areas of ALL the faces.

SURFACE AREA OF A CUBE AND CUBOID	SURFACE AREA OF A CYLINDER
Find the area of each face and then add them together.	$2\pi r^2 + 2\pi rh$

SURFACE AREA OF A PYRAMID	SURFACE AREA OF A CONE
Add the area of the base to the sum of the areas of the triangular faces.	$\pi r^2 + \pi rl$

SURFACE AREA OF A SPHERE
$4\pi r^2$

DAY 3 ➡ **Geometry and Measures**

PLANS AND ELEVATIONS OF 3D SHAPES

PLANS and **ELEVATIONS** are 2D drawings of 3D shapes.

A **PLAN** is a drawing to scale which shows the shape as if you were looking directly down on it.

An **ELEVATION** is the view of the shape from the front or the side.

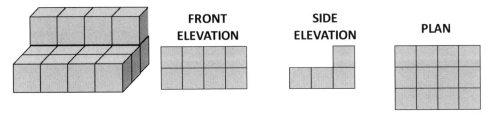

FRONT ELEVATION SIDE ELEVATION PLAN

Activity 4

Q1.

Below is a net of a cuboid.

The net shows the area of each face of the cuboid.

	18 cm²	
27 cm²	6 cm²	27 cm²	6 cm²
	18 cm²	

Work out the volume of the cuboid.

CIRCLES, SECTORS, AND ARCS

PI

Pi (π) is a number used to represent the ratio between the circumference and diameter of a circle.

$\pi = 3.14159265359...$

If you are sitting a calculator paper you can use the Pi button on your scientific calculator for accuracy.

If you are sitting a non-calculator paper you can use the estimation that $\pi = 3.14$

AREA AND CIRCUMFERENCE

AREA OF A CIRCLE	CIRCUMFERENCE OF A CIRCLE
πr^2	πd

RADIUS, DIAMETER AND CIRCUMFERENCE

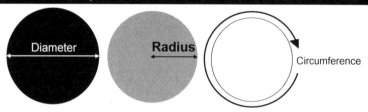

Diameter Radius Circumference

DIAMETER
The distance from one side of the circle to the other, passing through the center. This is twice the size of the radius.

RADIUS
The radius is half the length of the diameter. Starting from the middle of the circle, the radius reaches the edge of the circle.

CIRCUMFERENCE
The circumference is the outer edge of a circle.

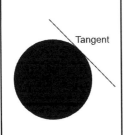	## TANGENT A tangent is a straight line which touches the outer side of the circle.
	## CHORD A chord is a straight line drawn across the inside of a circle, but does not run through the center (if it runs through the centre it is called the diameter).
	## SECTOR A sector is a 'piece' or 'slice'. Using the mid-point of the circle, create two straight lines which reach the edge of the circle. Sector area = angle ÷ 360° × πr^2.
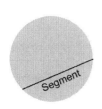	## SEGMENT A segment is the area you get when you draw a chord. The chord is the line, whereas the segment is the area in that chord.
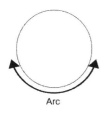	## ARC An arc is part of the circumference of the circle. Arc length = angle ÷ 360° × πd.

Activity 5

Q1.

Below is a circle. Find the circumference and the area to 1 decimal place.

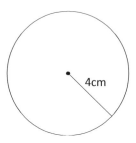

4cm

Q2.

Below is a semi-circle which has a diameter of 48 cm.

Work out the perimeter of the semi-circle.

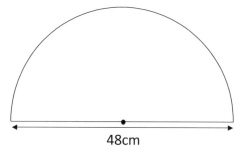

48cm

Q3.

Find the shaded area. Write your answer to 1 decimal place.

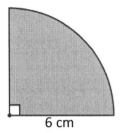

6 cm

TRANSFORMATIONS AND ENLARGEMENTS

You need to learn the four TRANSFORMATIONS when it comes to looking at shapes.

The four transformations that you need to know are:

1. Translations

2. Rotations

3. Reflections

4. Enlargements

TRANSLATIONS

When we talk about translating shapes, this basically means **SLIDING** the shape into a new position.

Translations are very easy to understand if you know how the shape has been moved. That is why we must **ALWAYS** say how far along and how far up (or down) the shape has moved.

We describe the movement of the shape using **VECTORS**.

<u>When describing the movement, you will:</u>

1. First describe the movement on the x axis (how many spaces the shape has moved left or right).

2. And then, describe the movement on the y axis (how many spaces the shape has moved up or down).

EXAMPLE

Take a look at the following grid. Triangles A, B and C have all been translated. But, we need to understand how each shape has moved across the page; to do this we will use vectors.

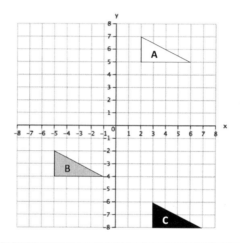

Step 1 = place a black dot on one of the corners on triangle A. Whichever corner of the triangle you have marked, do the same for triangles B and C.

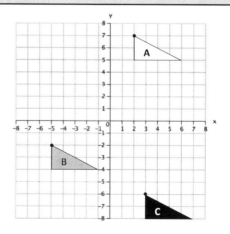

Step 2 = next, work out how triangle A translates to triangle B.

- Using the dotted corner on triangle A, first work out how the triangle has moved sideways.

  The triangle has moved 7 spaces to the left (which means the vector component would be −7).

- Next, work out how the triangle has moved up or down.

  The triangle has moved 9 spaces downwards (which means the vector component would be −9).

- So the translation by vector from A to B is $\begin{pmatrix} -7 \\ -9 \end{pmatrix}$

Step 3 = next, work out how triangle B translates to triangle C.

- Using the dotted corner on triangle B, first work out how the triangle has moved sideways.

  The triangle has moved 8 spaces to the right (which means the vector component would be 8).

- Next, work out how the triangle has moved up or down.

  The triangle has moved 4 spaces downwards (which means the vector component would be −4).

- So, the translation by vector from B to C is $\begin{pmatrix} 8 \\ -4 \end{pmatrix}$

REMEMBER

- Moving to the right or up – vector component will be **POSITIVE**.

- Moving to the left or down – vector component will be **NEGATIVE**.

- Describe the x axis first (right or left)

- Describe the y axis second (up or down)

ROTATIONS

Another way you can transform a shape is by **ROTATION.**

When describing a rotation, you will need to know:

1. The direction of rotation (clockwise or anti-clockwise).

2. The angle of rotation (90˚ or 180˚).

3. The centre of rotation - this can be the origin which is where the x-axis and y-axis meet.

EXAMPLE

Take a look at the following grid. Triangle A has been rotated to form triangle B.

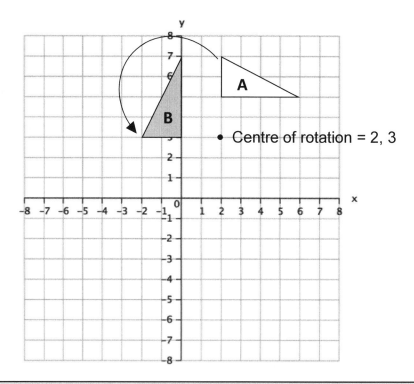

• Centre of rotation = 2, 3

In the above diagram, triangle A has been rotated 90˚ ANTI-CLOCKWISE.

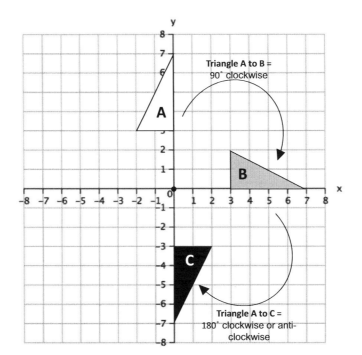

In the above diagram, we are using the centre rotation of (0, 0).

To get from triangle A to triangle B, we have rotated triangle A 90° clockwise.

If you wanted to get from triangle A to triangle C, we can rotate the triangle 180° using the centre rotation vectors. It does not matter whether you go clockwise or anti-clockwise, because you will end up in the same position!

REMEMBER

- Make sure you know the angle of rotation, direction of rotation and/ or the centre of rotation.

- A good way to practise these types of questions is to use **TRACING PAPER**.

- Know the difference between clockwise and anti-clockwise. Clockwise is the direction you will see the hands of a clock moving around in.

REFLECTIONS

Another transformation is using **REFLECTIONS**.

Think of shape reflections as a way of looking into a mirror. Using a mirror line, the object must appear exactly as it does on the other side.

The mirror line can be placed anywhere on an x and y grid.

EXAMPLE

Take a look at the following grids. Triangles A, B and C have all been reflected using mirror lines.

The dotted black lines represent mirrors!

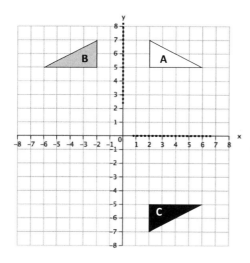 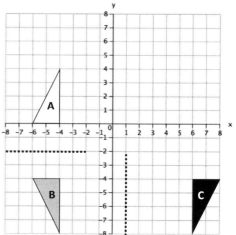

The diagram shows two reflections.

To get from triangle A to triangle B, we have reflected the shape using the y axis.

To get from the triangle A to triangle C, we have reflected the shape using the x axis.

In the diagram above, the mirror line between triangle A and triangle B is $y = -2$.

The mirror line between triangle B and triangle C is $x = 1$.

ENLARGEMENTS

ENLARGEMENTS are a way of transforming the size of a shape.

We can use a **SCALE FACTOR** to work out how the side lengths are changing.

For example, a scale factor of 2 means multiply each side by 2.

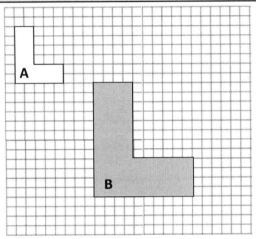

The enlargement of shape A to shape B has a scale factor of 2.

Each side length has been multiplied by 2.

When describing an enlargement, you need to focus on:

1. The scale factor.

2. The centre of enlargement.

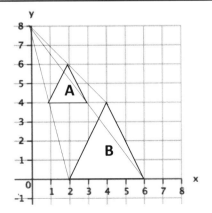

To work out the scale factor:

New length ÷ old length

So the enlargement which transforms triangle A to triangle B has a scale factor of 2.

The centre of enlargement is (0, 8).

To work out the centre of enlargement:

- Draw lines which go through the matching corners of each shape. So, draw a line going through the top corner of triangle A to the top corner of triangle B, and so forth.

- Wherever these lines meet, that is the centre of enlargement.

Activity 6

Q1.

a) Translate A using the vectors $\begin{pmatrix} -7 \\ -2 \end{pmatrix}$. Label the new shape 'B'.

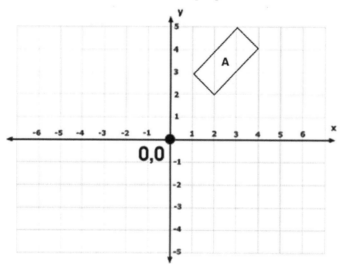

Q2.

a) Describe the type of transformation that maps shape A onto shape B.

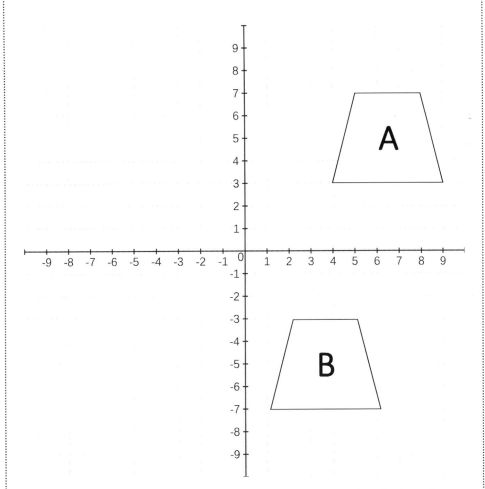

b) Rotate shape B 90° clockwise about the origin. Label the new shape 'C'.

c) Reflect shape C in the line $y = 1$. Label the new shape 'D'.

FINDING THE MISSING LENGTH OF SIMILAR SHAPES

Look at the two images below:

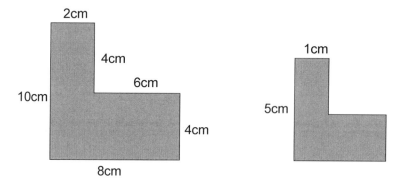

As you can see, the above shapes are similar, having lengths in the same ratio. The shape on the left is larger than the shape on the right.

Corresponding side lengths should be divided to find the scale factor and then use this to find the missing side lengths.

* $10 \div 5 = 2$

This means the scale factor is 2. We can check this using the other given lengths.

* $2 \div 1 = 1 = 2$

You can now use the scale factor to work out the missing lengths.

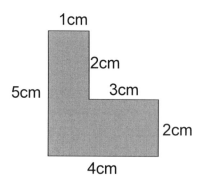

PYTHAGORAS' THEOREM

Pythagoras' Theorem can be used to find ANY length of a right angled triangle.

PYTHAGORAS' THEOREM FORMULA

$$a^2 + b^2 = c^2$$

When it comes to Pythagoras, there are a few things that you need to be aware of:

- Pythagoras' Theorem can only be applied to **RIGHT-ANGLED TRIANGLES**.

- Two sides of the triangle will always be known, and you will need to work out the third length.

- Make sure that your answer **LOOKS** sensible!

- The longest side of the triangle is called the **HYPOTENUSE**, and this side is always opposite the right angle.

- The square of the hypotenuse is equal to the sum of the squares of the other sides of the triangle.

If the sides of the triangle are labelled a, b and c, then use Pythagoras' theorem $c^2 = a^2 + b^2$

EXAMPLE 1

Find the length BC in the triangle. Write your answer to 2 decimal places.

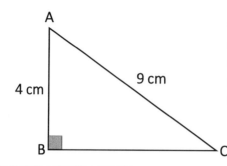

- $BC^2 + 4^2 = 9^2$
- $BC^2 + 16 = 81$
- $BC^2 = 81 - 16 = 65$
- $AB = 65 = \sqrt{8.0622}$ cm
- To 2 decimal places = 8.06 cm

EXAMPLE 2

Find the length BC in the triangle. Write your answer to 1 decimal place.

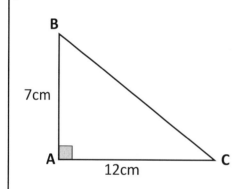

BC = hypotenuse

- $7^2 + 12^2 = BC^2$
- $49 + 144 = 193$
- $193 = BC^2$
- $BC = \sqrt{193} = 13.892$ cm
- To 1 decimal place = 13.9 cm

<u>Key things to remember:</u>

- If you are trying to find the longest side, you will ADD the two squared numbers.

- If you are trying to find one of the shorter sides, you will subtract the smaller squared side length from the larger squared side length.

- Square the two numbers you are given. There is a squared button on a calculator!

- Remember to find the square root! There is a square root button on a calculator!

Activity 7

Q1.

Work out the length of side A. Write your answer to 1 decimal place.

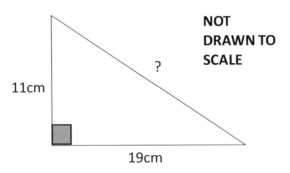

NOT DRAWN TO SCALE

11cm

?

19cm

Q2.

Calculate the scale factor then work out the length of DF. Write your answer to 1 decimal place.

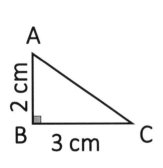

A

2 cm

B

3 cm

C

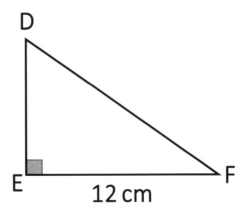

D

E

12 cm

F

DETERMINING RIGHT-ANGLES

Using Pythagoras' theorem, you can also work out whether or not a triangle contains a right-angle.

The best way to learn this is through example:

Question

Does the triangle ABC contain a right-angle?

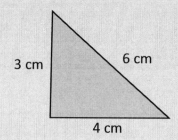

3 cm   6 cm

4 cm

- $3^2 + 4^2 = 9 + 16 = 25$

- The longest side of the triangle is 6cm.

- $6^2 = 36$

- 25 does not equal 36, therefore this triangle does not contain a right angle.

TRIGONOMETRY

Each one of the names above links two sides and an angle. Again, this only works with **RIGHT-ANGLED TRIANGLES.**

The hypotenuse = the longest side of the triangle.

The opposite = the opposite side to the angle being used (x)

The adjacent = is the other side next to the angle being used.

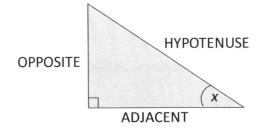

DON'T FORGET:
SOH   CAH   TOA

SOH	CAH	TOA
		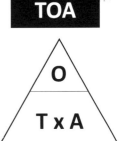

There are three formulas that you need to understand.

$$\text{Sin } x = \frac{Opposite}{Hypotenuse} \qquad \text{Cos } x = \frac{Adjacent}{Hypotenuse} \qquad \text{Tan } x = \frac{Opposite}{Adjacent}$$

Key things to remember:

- You use the side you are given and the side you are working out to determine the sin/cos/tan (O,H A,H or O,A).

- From that, you will be able to choose which formula you need to use to solve the question (**SOH, CAH, TOA**).

- Then using the formula, use the triangles above to show you how to correctly use each formula.

- Cover up the thing you are trying to find, and do the calculation that is left.

EXAMPLE

Work out the length of the opposite side. Give your answer to 1 decimal place.

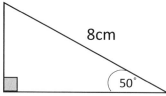

STEP 1

Label the sides.

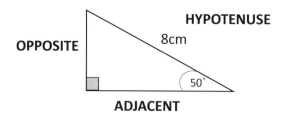

STEP 2

The opposite and the hypotenuse are involved, so the formula we will use is **SOH.**

STEP 3

We are trying to work out O, so cover it up and do the calculation:

= **s**in 50° × 8 = 6.12

To 1 decimal place = 6.1cm

LEARNING TO CALCULATE AN ANGLE

You can work out the angle of a triangle by using the formulas as previously shown.

Let's take a look at an example.

<u>Question</u>

Calculate the angle *XYZ*. Give your answer to 1 decimal place.

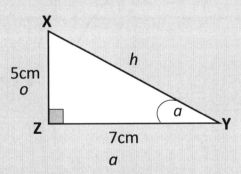

- First, label each side with *o*, *h* and *a*.

- In the triangle, you have been given the lengths of *o* and *a*.

- Tan × = $\dfrac{\text{opposite}}{\text{adjacent}}$

- Tan × = $\dfrac{5}{7}$ = 0.714285...

- Calculate the angle, using the inverse tan button: tan⁻¹:

- Angle *a* = 35.5°

ELEVATION AND DEPRESSION

This is all to do with angles. If someone stands and looks at an object, the **ANGLE OF ELEVATION** is between the line of horizontal sight, and the object.

If someone stands and looks down at an object, the **ANGLE OF DEPRESSION** is between the line of horizontal sight, and the object.

ANGLE OF ELEVATION

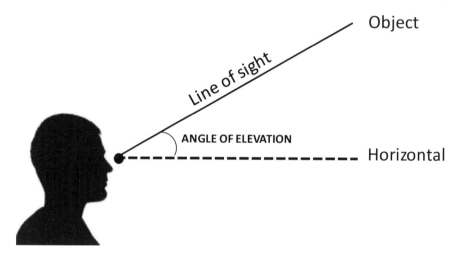

ANGLE OF DEPRESSION

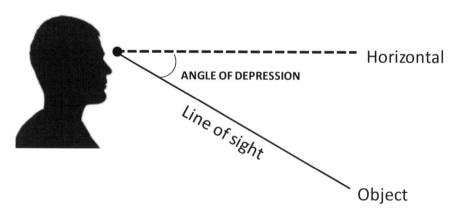

Let's take a look at a sample question involving elevation and depression.

Question

A man who is 1.8 metres tall, stands outside a building and looks up. He is standing 30 metres away from the base of the building, and is trying to work out the height of the building.

The angle of elevation to the top of the building is 50°. What is the height of the building? Give your answer to 1 decimal place.

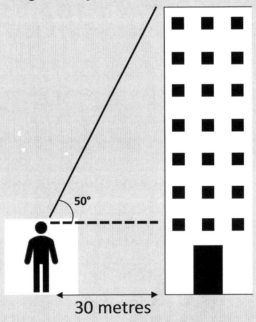

30 metres

- First, you need to label the sides *o*, *a* and *h*.

- In the triangle, we need to calculate the length of *o*.

- $o = 30 \times \tan 50$

- 35.8 metres (to 1 d.p.).

- 35.8 + 1.8 (the height of the man) means the height of the building is 37.6 metres.

Activity 8

Q1.

Find the length of AC. Write your answer to 1 decimal place.

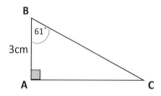

Q2.

From the top of the 12 metres high vertical tree, the person has an angle of depression of 35°. How far away is the person from the base of the tree? Give your answer to 1 decimal place.

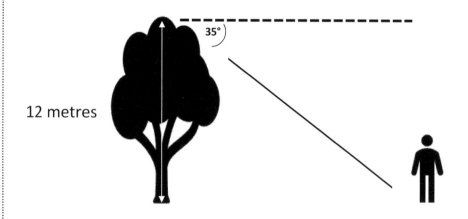

VECTORS

A **VECTOR** describes a movement from one point to another.

A **VECTOR QUANTITY** has both magnitude and direction.

A **SCALAR QUANTITY** only has magnitude.

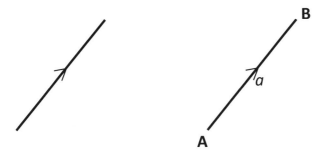

Between Point A and Point B, this can be written as:

AB , **a** *or* **a̲**.

You can represent vectors by using columns.

For example,

- This basically says, 'go along the x axis once, and up the y axis five times'.

You can also have negative vectors. This will have the same magnitude, but in the opposite direction. You would just put a minus sign in front to show the change in direction (z) and (-z).

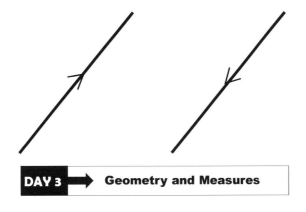

DAY 3 ➡ **Geometry and Measures**

If two vectors are equal, they will be parallel and equal in length.

* $\overrightarrow{AB}$ is equal to **a**.

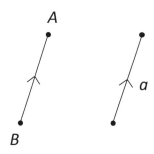

If $\overrightarrow{DE}$ = k$\overrightarrow{AB}$, then $\overrightarrow{AB}$ and $\overrightarrow{DE}$ are parallel and the length of $\overrightarrow{DE}$ is k times the length of $\overrightarrow{AB}$.

$$\overrightarrow{AB} = \begin{pmatrix} 4 \\ 2 \end{pmatrix}$$

$$\overrightarrow{DE} = \begin{pmatrix} 8 \\ 4 \end{pmatrix} = 2\begin{pmatrix} 4 \\ 2 \end{pmatrix}$$

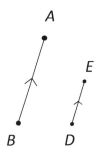

Activity 9

Q1.

Below is a sketch.

A is the point (4, 2)

B is the point (5, 5)

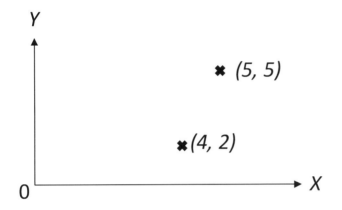

Write down the vector **AB**.

Write down your answer as a column vector. $\begin{pmatrix} x \\ y \end{pmatrix}$

LOCI

The locus of a point is the set of all possible positions determined by one or more rules or conditions.

TYPES OF LOCI

CIRCLE

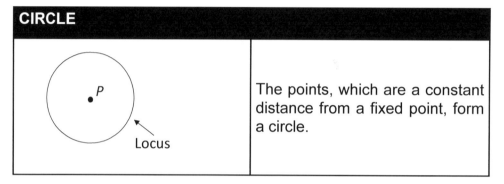

The points, which are a constant distance from a fixed point, form a circle.

PERPENDICULAR BISECTOR

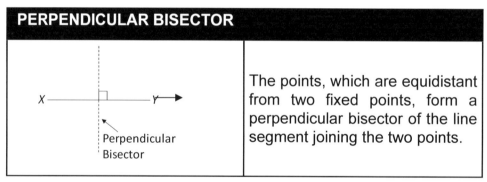

The points, which are equidistant from two fixed points, form a perpendicular bisector of the line segment joining the two points.

PARALLEL LINES

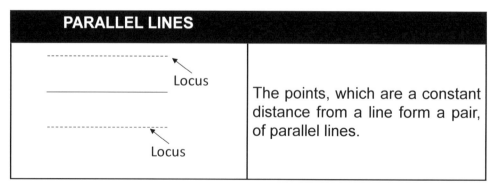

The points, which are a constant distance from a line form a pair, of parallel lines.

ANGLE BISECTOR

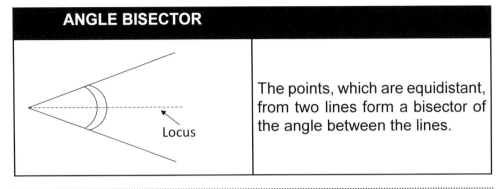

Locus

The points, which are equidistant, from two lines form a bisector of the angle between the lines.

Activity 10

Q1.

Below is a rectangle that has been accurately drawn.

Shade the set of points inside the rectangle which meet all of the conditions below:

- The distance between each point and *C* is more than 2.5cm.

- The distance between each point and the line *AD* is more than 2cm.

CONSTRUCTIONS

To construct, you will need a pair of compasses and a ruler.

CONSTRUCTING A TRIANGLE

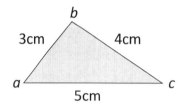 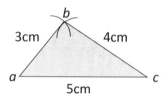

- First, draw the longest side ac.

- With your compass at point a, draw an arc of radius 3cm.

- With your compass at point c, draw an arc of radius 4cm.

- Join a and c to the point where the two arcs meet at c.

CONSTRUCTING A PERPENDICULAR BISECTOR

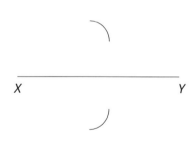 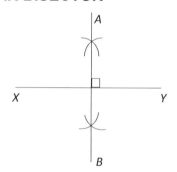

- Draw line XY.

- Draw two arcs using X as the centre. The pair of compasses must be set at a greater distance than half of XY.

- Draw two arcs using Y as the centre. Draw a line connecting the two meeting points of the arcs. This is your perpendicular bisector.

BISECTING AN ANGLE

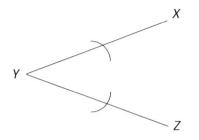 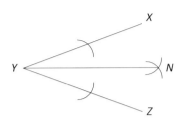

- Draw two lines (XY) and (YZ)
- Use a pair of compasses, and place the point on Y.
- Draw arcs on XY and YZ.
- Place the compass point at the two arcs XY and YZ to create a point at N.
- Join YN to bisect your angle.

Activity II

Q1.

Using only a ruler and a pair of compasses, bisect this angle.

You must show all construction lines.

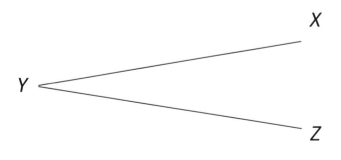

ANSWERS TO DAY 3

ANGLES

ACTIVITY I

Q1. 125°

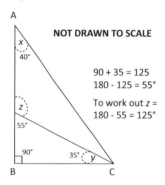

A

NOT DRAWN TO SCALE

x

40°

z

55°

90°

35° *y*

B

C

90 + 35 = 125
180 - 125 = 55°

To work out *z* =
180 - 55 = 125°

Q2. 94°

Opposite angles (indicated by the dotted line) are the same.

The isosceles triangle (indicated by the dashes on two of the lines) means that the two angles are the same.

Therefore 180 – 47 – 47 = 86°.
180 – 86 = 94°.

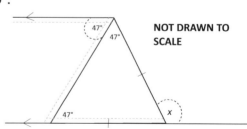

47°
47°
47°
x

NOT DRAWN TO
SCALE

Q3.

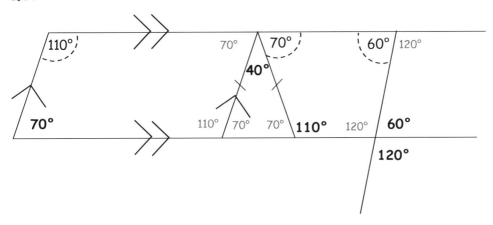

A = 70° - A parallelogram contains two pairs of equal angles, which add to 360°

B = 40° - Angles on a straight line add up to 180°. Angles in a triangle add up to 360°

C = 110° - Angles on a straight line add up to 180°

D = 60° - Corresponding angles are equal.

E = 120° - Alternate angles are equal.

LINES

ACTIVITY 2

Q1. 5

Q2. A and C

- Only the lines A and C are perpendicular to one another.

2D SHAPES

ACTIVITY 3

Q1.

Name of shape	No. of sides	Lines of symmetry
Square	4	4
Regular Hexagon	6	6
Regular Octagon	8	8
Regular Heptagon	7	7

Q2.

- Regular Nonagon = 9 lines of symmetry

- Equilateral Triangle = 3 lines of symmetry

- Regular Octagon = 8 lines of symmetry

Q3.

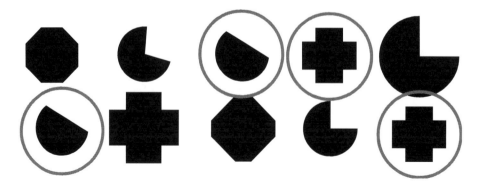

3D SHAPES

ACTIVITY 4

18 cm²

9 cm | 2 cm

27 cm² | 6 cm² | 27 cm² | 3 cm | 6 cm²

18 cm²

Q1. 54cm³

- Volume = height × width × length
- 2 × 9 × 3 = 54

CIRCLES, SECTORS, AND ARCS

ACTIVITY 5

Q1. Circumference = 25.1 cm and Area = 50.3 cm²

- Circumference = $\pi \times 8 = 25.13274...$
- Area = $\pi \times 4^2 = 50.26548...$

Q2. 123.4 cm

- $\frac{1}{2} (\pi \times 48) + 48 = 123.39822...$

Q3. 28.3 cm²

- Area of a circle = πr^2
- Quarter of a circle = $(\pi r^2) \div 4$
- Radius = 6 cm
- Area = $(\pi \times 6^2) \div 4 = 36\pi \div 4 = 28.3 \text{cm}^2$ (1 d.p.)

DAY 3 ➡ **Geometry and Measures**

TRANSFORMATIONS AND ENLARGEMENTS

ACTIVITY 6

Q1.

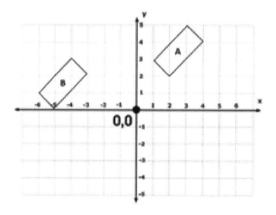

Q2. a) Translation

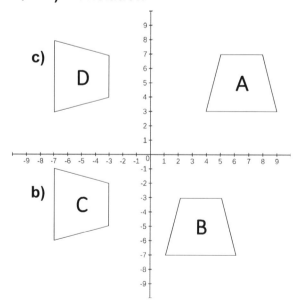

PYTHAGORAS' THEOREM

ACTIVITY 7

Q1. 22 cm

- $11^2 = 121$
- $19^2 = 361$
- $121 + 361 = 482$
- $\sqrt{482} = 21.9544$
- To one decimal place = 22.0

Q2. 14.4 cm

- $12 \div 3 = 4$ (scale factor)
- $a^2 + b^2 = DF^2$
- $8^2 + 12^2 = DF^2$
- $64 + 144 = DF^2$
- $208 = DF^2$
- $DF = \sqrt{208}$
- $DF = 14.42220$
- To one decimal place = 14.4

TRIGONOMETRY

ACTIVITY 8

Q1. 5.4cm

* AC is opposite to the angle given and AB is adjacent to it.

* $3 \times \tan61 = 5.412$

* To 1 decimal place = 5.4cm

Q2. 17.1 metres

* In the triangle, the height (o) is known. We need to work out the length of the adjacent (a).

* $\text{Tan} \times = \dfrac{\text{opposite}}{\text{adjacent}}$

* $\text{Tan } 35 = \dfrac{12}{y}$

* Rearrange the equation, to make y the subject:

* $y \times \tan35 = 12$

* $y = \dfrac{12}{\tan35}$

* $y = 17.137776...$ metres

TRIGONOMETRY

ACTIVITY 9

Q1.

$$\begin{pmatrix} 1 \\ 3 \end{pmatrix}$$

LOCI

ACTIVITY 10

Q1.

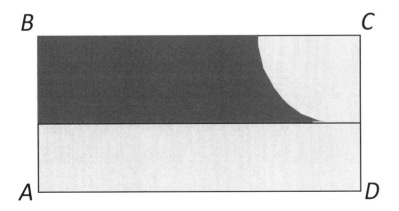

CONSTRUCTIONS

ACTIVITY II

Q1.

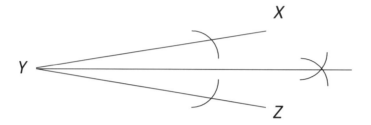

Day 3 Checklist

You have now completed your Day 3 revision.

How confident are you feeling?

Below we have included a checklist that you can tick off to make sure that you have learnt everything regarding this chapter.

I have read and understood the examples for tackling different geometry and measure calculations.

I have tackled all of the questions in this section.

I have read and understood the answers in this section.

I feel confident in Geometry and Measures questions.

PROBABILITY AND STATISTICS

Day 4

PROBABILITY AND PROBABILITY SCALES

Probability is all about estimating how likely (probable) an event is to happen. It is the 'maths of chance'.

Below we have outlined some 'events' where you'll need to use probability to estimate how likely something is to happen:

- The odds of a coin landing on heads (or tails);
- The odds of a die landing on a particular number;
- The odds of it raining in the first week of December.

When we think about probability, we are basically saying 'what are the chances?'

When looking at probabilities, there are several rules to remember:

- If there is only one possible result, then it will have a probability of 1 (it is certain to happen).
- If there is a 0.24 chance of something happening, there is a 0.76 chance of it NOT happening (1 − 0.24 = 0.76).
- In any scenario, the probabilities of all the possible outcomes will add up to 1. So if you know the probability of something happening, you can subtract that probability from 1 to find the probability of it NOT happening.

Below we have created a probability scale to demonstrate how to use them.

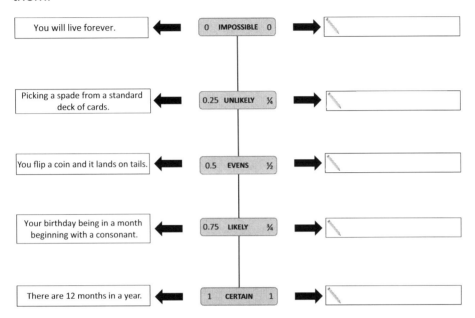

You will live forever.	0 IMPOSSIBLE 0	
Picking a spade from a standard deck of cards.	0.25 UNLIKELY ¼	
You flip a coin and it lands on tails.	0.5 EVENS ½	
Your birthday being in a month beginning with a consonant.	0.75 LIKELY ¾	
There are 12 months in a year.	1 CERTAIN 1	

EQUAL CHANCE	UNEQUAL CHANCE
The probability of something which has the same level of chance, is known as **'EQUAL PROBABILITY'**. We can demonstrate this with two examples. **1. Throwing a die** You have an equal chance of landing on an even number as you do an odd number. **2. Tossing a coin** You have an equal chance of the coin landing on heads as it does tails.	The probability of something which has different levels of chance, is known as **'UNEQUAL PROBABILITY'**. For example: If you have a bag of 10 buttons (3 are red, 2 are blue, 1 is orange, and the rest are yellow) you have different chances of picking out different coloured buttons. **FORMULA** To work out the probability: *Number of ways something can happen* ――――――――――――――――― *Total number of possible outcomes*

RELATIVE FREQUENCY

Relative frequency is determining the likely outcome of something.

Theoretical probability is what you EXPECT to happen. Experimental probability is what ACTUALLY happens.

Ethan throws a die. He is trying to work out the probability of the die landing on the number 4. Ethan says:

"The probability that the die lands on a 4 is 1 out of 6 ($\frac{1}{6}$). That means if I throw the die 6 times, I should get exactly one 4."

Theoretically, Ethan is correct. However, if Ethan runs this experiment, this might not be the case. You won't always get exactly one 4.

If Ethan rolls the die 24 times, how many times can Ethan expect the die to land on the number 2?

• If there is a 1 in 6 chance of the die landing on the number 2, this means that for every roll, Ethan has the same chance.

• In 24 rolls, Ethan can expect to roll the number 2 four times.

• Every time Ethan repeats this experiment, his results will of course change!

IF WE FLIPPED 2 COINS, WHAT ARE THE OUTCOMES?

- There are four possible outcomes:

  HH   HT   TH   TT

- The probability of two coins both landing on heads is ¼.
- The probability of two coins both landing on tails is ¼.
- The probability of two coins landing on heads then tails is ¼.
- The probability of two coins landing on tails then heads is ¼.

Activity I

Q1.

Rachel has a bag of buttons. Each button has a number.

6	5	9	4	1	3	6
5	7	9	8	2	5	5
6	9	1	2	9	4	6
3	7	9	5	4	1	2

Rachel picks a button out of a bag at random. What is the probability of picking the following? Simplify your answers.

a) P(odd number) =

b) P(even number) =

c) P(number $\leq$ 5) =

d) P(number $\geq$ 5) =

Probability trees, or frequency trees, are a GREAT way to record and organise data using frequencies. This allows you to work out the probabilities.

Let's take a look at an example.

In a dance show, there are 120 dancers in total. 87 of the dancers are female. 58 of the 87 female dancers are under 18. 16 of the male dancers are over 18.

- There are 120 dancers in total. 87 of the dancers are female.

- That means there are 33 male dancers.

- 58 of the 87 female dancers are under 18. That means 29 of the female dancers are over 18.

- 16 of the 33 male dancers are over 18. That means there are 17 male dancers under the age of 18.

- This is what your frequency tree should look like:

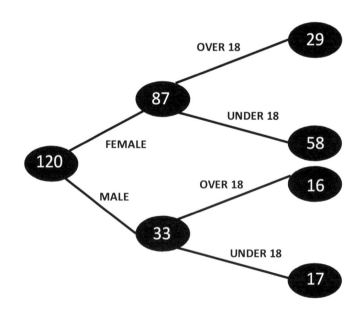

Activity 2

Q1.

In a bag, there are two colour marbles – orange and green. There are 7 orange marbles and 5 green marbles.

Sammie takes a marble out of the bag at random. She keeps the marble out of the bag.

She then takes a second marble from the bag. Complete the probability tree diagram.

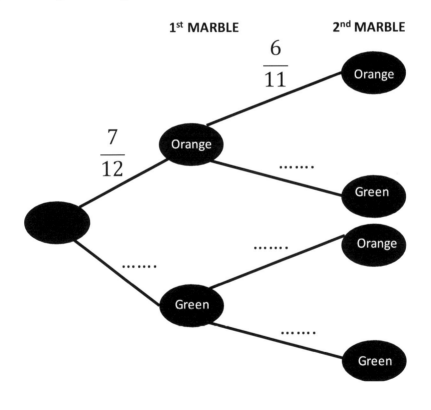

MEAN, MODE, MEDIAN AND RANGE

HOW TO WORK OUT THE MEAN

The **MEAN** is the most common form of average.
To calculate the mean all you need to do is **ADD UP** all of the numbers, and then **DIVIDE** the sum by how many numbers there are.

MEAN = SUM OF NUMBERS ÷ AMOUNT OF NUMBERS

| 6 | 9 | 12 | 21 | 34 | 27 | 23 | 20 |

To work out the mean:

STEP 1 – Add up all of the numbers.
6 + 9 + 12 + 21 + 34 + 27 + 23 + 20 = 152

STEP 2 – Divide the sum by how many numbers there are.
152 ÷ 8 = 19

HOW TO WORK OUT THE MODE

The **MODE** is the value that occurs
the most number of times.
This is the **ONLY** average that can have multiple values.

MODE = MOST COMMON

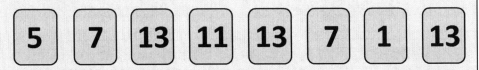

To work out the mode:

STEP 1 – rearrange the numbers in ascending order.
1   5   7   7   11   13   13   13

STEP 2 – What number occurs the most?
13 appears 3 times so this is the mode.

HOW TO WORK OUT THE MEDIAN

The **MEDIAN** is the number in the middle, after you've arranged the numbers in ascending order.

MEDIAN = MIDDLE

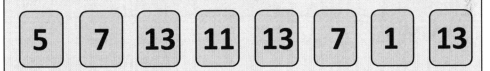

To work out the median:

STEP 1 – rearrange the numbers in ascending order.
1   5   7   7   11   13   13   13

STEP 2 – What number is in the middle?
The numbers 7 and 11 are in the middle. To work out the middle number, add up the numbers and then divide it by how many numbers there are: 7 + 11 = 18, then, 18 ÷ 2 = 9. So, 9 is the median.

HOW TO WORK OUT THE RANGE

The **RANGE** is the difference between the highest value and the lowest value.

To work out the range, subtract the lowest value from the highest value.

HIGHEST VALUE – LOWEST VALUE

| 5 | 7 | 13 | 11 | 13 | 7 | 1 | 13 |

To work out the range:

STEP 1 – subtract the lowest number from the highest number.

13 – 1 = 12

So the range for this set of data is 12.

Activity 3

Q1.

Find the mean, mode, median, and range for this set of data.

| 26 | 10 | 12 | 15 | 17 | 22 | 10 |

BARS

One of the easiest ways to display data is through the use of a BAR CHART.

Bars are used on a graph to show the frequency of something (i.e. how many).

Let's take a look at an example. Below are three paragraphs. Work out whether they were written by the same person.

Paragraph 1

A tramp, and a hard looking one, said Ben to himself.
He hesitated about answering, being naturally reluctant to have such a traveling companion.
"Well, what do you say?" demanded the tramp rather impatiently.
"There's plenty of room on that seat, and I'm dead tired."
"Where are you going?"
"Same way you are, to Pentonville."
"You can ride," said Ben.

Paragraph 2

First he went to the barn and filled one pocket
you see, he was a big boy now and had pockets
one, two, three, four, five, six, seven
one over his heart, two close by his belt, one on the inside of his jacket
one on each side of his hips and two in the back of his corduroy trousers.

Paragraph 3

Dick led the way, and the gentleman followed him into the store.
At the reappearance of Dick in such company, the clerk blushed a little, and looked nervous.
He fancied that he could browbeat a youngster, but with a gentleman he saw that it would be a different matter. He turned around and began replacing some goods on the shelves.

The way to do it is to take one paragraph at a time and count how many words have just one letter, how many words have just two letters, and so on.

Start with paragraph 1. There are 3 words with 1 letter, there are 8 words with 2 letters and there are 15 words with 3 letters. But there is a better way of writing this down.

Something called a frequency table is used. Frequency is a word that means 'how often something happens'. In paragraph 1, the frequency of 2 letter words is 8. In other words 2 letter words happen 8 times.

Frequency table for paragraph 1

Word length	1	2	3	4	5	6	7	8	9	10	11	12
Frequency	3	8	15	15	5	3	2	1	5	0	2	0

Check that the table is correct. Are there 13 words with 4 letters and 3 words with 6 letters? Check it all, and, when you are happy with it draw a bar chart.

Bar Chart for Paragraph 1

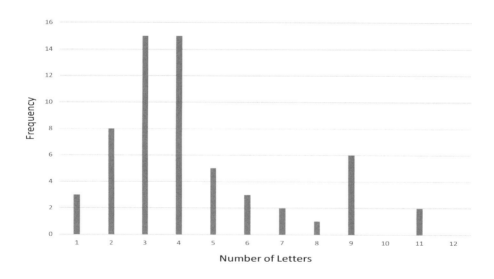

Now do the same thing for the other two paragraphs.

| DAY 4 ➡ | Probability and Statistics |

It will be possible to see which two were written by the same person because two of the bar charts will have almost the same shape but the other one will be different.

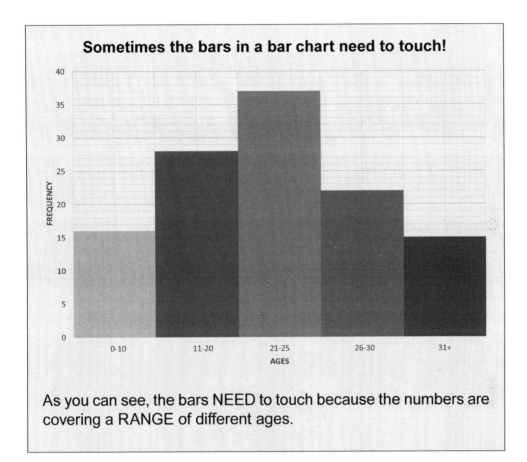

Sometimes the bars in a bar chart need to touch!

As you can see, the bars NEED to touch because the numbers are covering a RANGE of different ages.

COMPOSITE BAR GRAPHS

Here is a bar chart showing which subject girls and boys preferred.

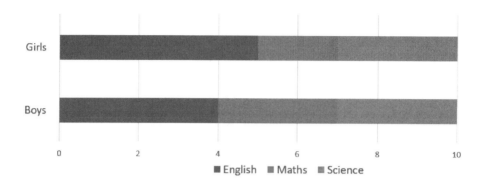

- In the above composite bar graph, the following information is displayed:

- 5 girls preferred English, 2 girls preferred Maths, and 3 girls preferred Science.

- 4 boys preferred English, 3 boys preferred Maths, and 3 boys preferred Science.

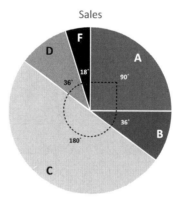

In order to work out the size of each sector of the pie chart, you need to work out what angle needs to represent each sector.

GRADE	A	B	C	D	F
FREQUENCY	25	10	50	10	5

STEP 1

Add up the total number of people.

$$25 + 10 + 50 + 10 + 5 = 100$$

STEP 2

Next, you will need to work out the fraction of the total for each grade.

- Grade A = $^{25}/_{100}$
- Grade B = $^{10}/_{100}$
- Grade C = $^{50}/_{100}$
- Grade D = $^{10}/_{100}$
- Grade F = $^{5}/_{100}$

STEP 3

Multiply each fraction by 360°.

- Grade A = 25 ÷ 100 × 360° = 90°
- Grade B = 10 ÷ 100 × 360° = 36°
- Grade C = 50 ÷ 100 × 360° = 180°
- Grade D = 10 ÷ 100 × 360° = 36°
- Grade F = 5 ÷ 100 × 360° = 18° So, you now have the angles of each segment.

SCATTER

Understanding the correlation!

Scatter graphs are diagrams which analyse multiple sets of data.

They show the relationship between two variables, which makes it easier to analyse the data provided.

The link between the two variables is also called **CORRELATION**.

If the two variables are related in some way, you should be able to draw a **STRAIGHT LINE** through the middle of the points.

This straight line does not have to go through every single point on the scatter graph, but must pass most of the points closely.

This straight line is also known as **'THE LINE OF BEST FIT'**.

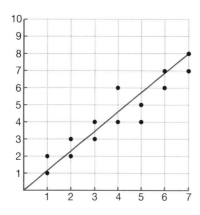

POSITIVE CORRELATION

The points must slant uphill (from left to right). This means that both variables either increase or decrease together.

You can draw a straight line through the plotted data. Dots need to be placed fairly evenly either side of the straight line.

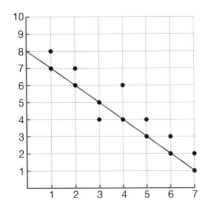

NEGATIVE CORRELATION

This means that the points slope downwards (from left to right). As one variable increases, the other decreases.

You can draw a line of best fit through the plotted data.

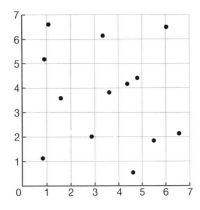

NO CORRELATION

No correlation means that the points are scattered all over the place, and therefore you are unable to draw a line of best fit.

This means that the two variables show no relation.

STRONG POSITIVE CORRELATION   **WEAK POSITIVE CORRELATION**

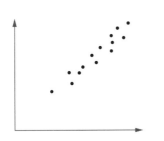 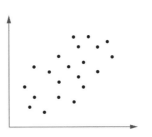

STRONG NEGATIVE CORRELATION   **WEAK NEGATIVE CORRELATION**

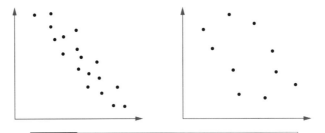

DAY 4 ➡ **Probability and Statistics**

LINE

A line graph is used to represent data over a specific amount of time.

It is often used to show **TRENDS**.

Instead of using bars like a bar chart, a line graph uses lines by plotting points and drawing lines between pairs of consecutive points.

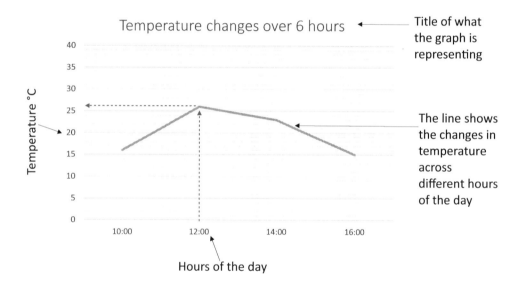

Work out the temperature at 12:00

Step 1 = draw an arrow from 12:00 all the way until you reach the line.
Step 2 = then read along that line and see what number it is.
Step 3 = the answer is 26 °C .

DAY 4 ➡ **Probability and Statistics**

FREQUENCIES

Frequency basically means:

'THE NUMBER OF TIMES SOMETHING OCCURS'.

Using tables is a great way to keep track of collected data.

You will normally have a category column, a tally column (optional), and a frequency column.

This will allow you to quickly see how many are in each category.

CATEGORIES

TRANSPORT	FREQUENCY
Car	22
Train	13
Bus	38
Walk	8
Cycle	17

HOW MANY IN EACH CATEGORY

Sometimes, instead of having just individual categories, you will have what are called **GROUPED FREQUENCIES**.

Group frequencies are data that can be put into classes.

INEQUALITIES often occur in data that doesn't always deal with whole numbers.

INEQUALITIES
The number 5 would be recorded in the top row, but the number 5.1 would be recorded in the second row.

HEIGHT	FREQUENCY
$0 < h \leq 5$	4
$5 < h \leq 10$	10
$10 < h \leq 15$	2
$15 < h \leq 20$	5

$\leq$
This sign means 'equal to or less than'.

DAY 4 ➡ **Probability and Statistics**

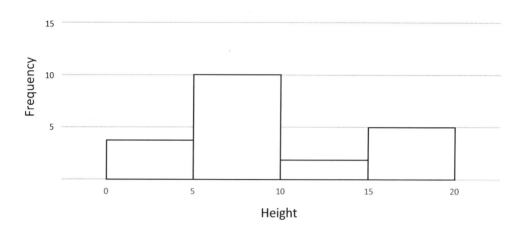

See how the bars in this chart have no gaps.

This is because the groups of classes have no gaps. In simpler terms, because the data deals with whole numbers and inequalities, there cannot be any gaps between the bars, as the data is flowing straight from one class to another.

Instead of drawing bar charts, you can also use **FREQUENCY POLYGONS**.

However, this is slightly trickier and you must remember this rule:

YOU MUST ALWAYS PLOT YOUR DATA AT THE MID-INTERVAL VALUE OF A CLASS/CATEGORY.

EXAMPLE

HEIGHT	0 ≤ h < 5	5 ≤ h < 10	10 ≤ h < 15	15 ≤ h < 20
Frequency	4	10	2	5
Mid-interval value	2.5	7.5	12.5	17.5

- 0 + 5 = 5   5 ÷ 2 = 2.5

- 5 + 10 = 15   15 ÷ 2 = 7.5

- 10 + 15 = 25   25 ÷ 2 = 12.5

- 15 + 20 = 35   35 ÷ 2 = 17.5

Remember the mid-interval value.

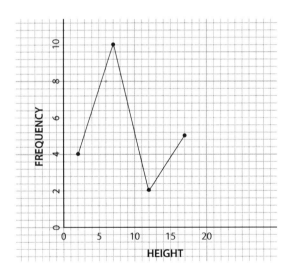

FREQUENCY TABLES, MODAL CLASS, AND MEAN VALUE

Calculating the modal class from a group of data (often in a frequency table), is relatively simple if you know the process.

EXAMPLE

Below shows a table of children's weight.

Mass (m) in kg	Frequency
$30 \leq m < 40$	8
$40 \leq m < 50$	4
$50 \leq m < 60$	2
$60 \leq m < 70$	2

To find the mean:

Mass (m) in kg	Midpoint	Frequency	Midpoint × Frequency
$30 \leq m < 40$	35	8	280
$40 \leq m < 50$	45	4	180
$50 \leq m < 60$	55	2	110
$60 \leq m < 70$	65	2	130

- 280 + 180 + 110 + 130 = 700
- 700 ÷ 16 = 43.75 kg.

To find the modal class:

- The modal class is the class that has the highest frequency.
- $30 \leq m < 40$ has the highest frequency, so therefore is the modal class.

DAY 4 ➡ **Probability and Statistics**

TALLIES

TALLY CHARTS are all about keeping count!

Frequency tables often use tallies to keep track of who chooses what category, before all of the data is added together. The tally part to a frequency graph is often left off recorded data (you can finalise the tallies with a simple 'frequency total').

Tally marks will look like this:

> Once you get to 4, the next tally mark will cross off the 4 marks (to make 5). This makes it easier to count the totals.

| 1 | 2 | 3 | 4 | 5 |

Colours	Tally	Frequency
Pink	JHT JHT JHT III	18
Blue	JHT JHT	10
Red	JHT IIII	9
Orange	JHT II	7
Green	JHT JHT II	12

Remember, FREQUENCY is another word for TOTAL.

PICTOGRAMS

Pictograms use PICTURES to represent data.

In order for a pictogram to work, you must have a KEY.

EXAMPLE

Five people counted the number of balloons they were able to pop in 30 seconds. Here are their results.

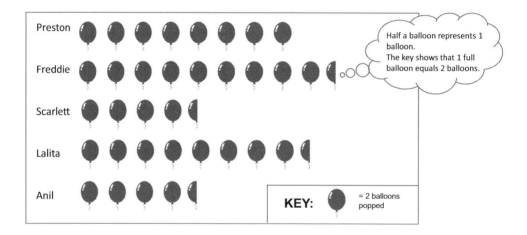

From the key, we can see that 1 picture of a balloon represents 2 balloons.

So, half a balloon represents 1 balloon.

HISTOGRAMS

The important thing to remember about histograms is not the height of each bar, but the AREA.

The area of the bar represents the frequency of the data.

EXAMPLE

The table below shows the age groups of people who learn to play a musical instrument.

Age	Frequency
5-10	18
11-15	5
16-17	6

You now need to find the class width for each of the categories.

Age	Frequency	Class Width
5-10	18	5
11-15	5	4
16-17	6	1

To work out the height of each bar, you need to divide frequency by the class width.

Age	Frequency	Class Width	Frequency Density
5-10	18	5	3.6
11-15	5	4	1.25
16-17	6	1	1

Once you have collected all of the information, you are then able to draw the histogram.

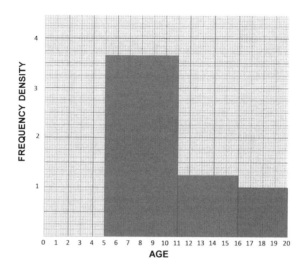

TYPES OF DATA

SET	A collection of objects, which are called the elements of the set. (The numbers 1 to 100 are a set).
SUBSET	A subset is a set which is part of a larger set. For example (2,3,4) is a subset of (1,2,3,4,5).
FINITE SET	A set which contains a finite amount of numbers, for example (2,4,6,8,10).
INFINITE SET	A set which contains an infinite amount of numbers, such as all the positive odd numbers (1,3,5,7,…).
EMPTY OR NULL SET	A set that contains no members. (ø)
UNIVERSAL SET	A set that contains all possible members.
UNION OF SETS	A set which contains all of the numbers which are members of one or both of two sets A and B. This is written as A ∪ B.
INTERSECTION OF SETS	A set which contains all of the numbers which belong to both of two sets A and B. This is written as A ∩ B.

Activity 4

Q1.

Draw a bar chart to represent the different motorway speed limits, based on country.

Belgium	74 mph
Netherlands	62 mph
Luxembourg	75 mph
Spain	80 mph
France	86 mph
Britain	70 mph
Germany	80 mph
Portugal	62 mph

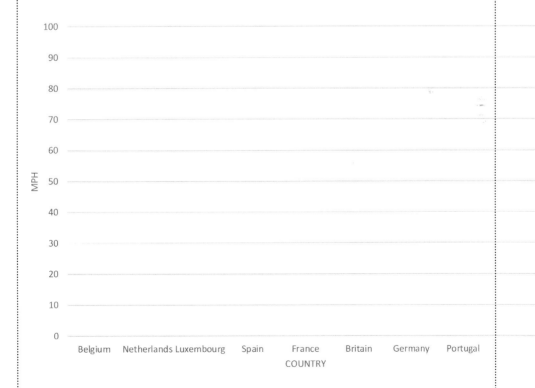

Q2.

The following table shows the number of cars that entered a local car park within a 30 minute period.

Number of cars	Frequency	No. of cars x frequency
1	3	
2	11	
3	12	
4	24	
5	24	
6	8	

a) Calculate the mode.

b) Calculate the range.

c) Calculate the median.

ANSWERS TO DAY 4

PROBABILITY

ACTIVITY 1

Q1.

a) P(odd number) = $^{17}/_{28}$

b) P(even number) = $^{11}/_{28}$

c) P(number ≤ 5) = $^{4}/_{7}$

d) P(number ≥ 5) = $^{17}/_{28}$

ACTIVITY 2

Q1.

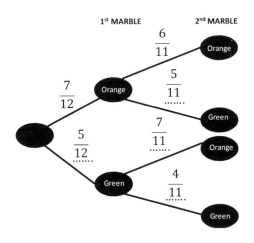

MEAN, MODE, MEDIAN, AND RANGE

ACTIVITY 3

Q1.

Mean = 16

- 26 + 10 + 12 + 15 + 17 + 22 + 10 = 112

- 112 ÷ 7 = 16

Mode = 10

- The number '10' occurs the most number of times in this set of data,

Median = 15

- 10   10   12   15   17   22   26

- The number '15' is in the middle.

Range = 16

- Largest number = 26

- Smallest number = 10

- 26 - 10 = 16

TYPES OF DATA

ACTIVITY 4

Q1.

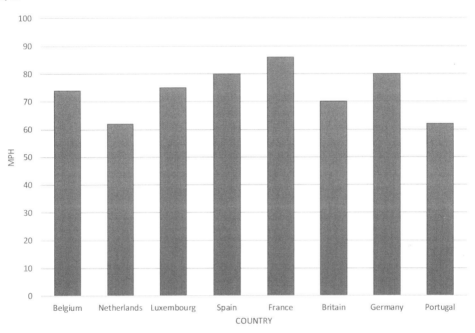

Q2.

a) 4 and 5 cars

- Both these categories have the value 24.

b) 6

- Highest value minus the lowest value = 6 − 1 = 5

c) 4

- Frequency total is 82. The middle numbers are 41 and 42. These numbers would occur in the fourth category (number of cars 4). So therefore the median is 4.

Day 4 Checklist

You have now completed your Day 4 revision.

How confident are you feeling?

Below we have included a checklist that you can tick off to make sure that you have learnt everything regarding this chapter.

I have read and understood the examples for tackling different probability and statistics calculations. ☐

I have tackled all of the questions in this section. ☐

I have read and understood the answers in this section. ☐

I feel confident in Probability and Statistics questions. ☐

ALGEBRA

Day 5

ALGEBRAIC EXPRESSIONS

When it comes to algebra, letters and/or symbols can be used to represent numbers.

TERM = A term is a single number, letter or product (multiplication) of numbers and letters.

- x x^2 $8x^3$

EXPRESSION = An expression is a short algebraic statement made up of one or more terms.

- $3x - 2$ $xy - x$

EQUATION = An equation is formed by setting two expressions to be equal to one another, by placing an equals sign between them.

- $3x + 4 = 10$

EXAMPLE

A rectangle has a width of x cm. The height is 4 cm less than the width. Write an expression for the perimeter.

- To work out the perimeter of a rectangle, we need to add up all of the sides.

- Perimeter $= x + x + (x - 4) + (x - 4)$

SIMPLIFYING EXPRESSIONS

Simplifying expressions, also known as collecting "like" terms, allows you to make the expression easier to read.

EXAMPLE

As you can see, the first term does not have an operation shown. However, this means that there is an INVISIBLE + sign.

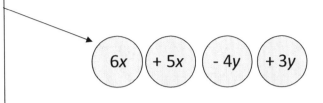

Using the expression in the above example, you can see that there are two different expressions - the terms that have the letter '***x***', and the terms that have the letter '***y***'.

That means we can simplify the expression as follows:

- The '*x*' terms can be collected together to give 11*x*.

- The '*y*' terms can be collected together to give -1*y*.

The easiest way to simplify expressions, is to group each term using brackets:

- $(6x)\ (+5x)\ (-4y)\ (+3y)$

EXPANDING BRACKETS

Multiplying brackets is quite a tricky thing to get your head around.

There are a few things that you can learn to make your life easier when it comes to multiplying out brackets:

1. The most important thing to remember is that everything **INSIDE** the bracket should be multiplied by the term (or number) **OUTSIDE** of the bracket.

2. If there is a minus sign **OUTSIDE** of the bracket, that will **REVERSE** all of the signs when multiplying.

EXAMPLE 1

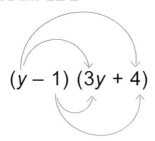

$3(a + b) + 2(a + b)$
- $(3a + 3b) + (2a + 2b)$
- $5a + 5b$

EXAMPLE 2

$(y - 1)\ (3y + 4)$

- $(y \times 3y) + (y \times 4) + (-1 \times 3y) + (-1 \times 4)$

  $\quad\ \ \textbf{3y}^2 \qquad\quad \textbf{+ 4y} \qquad\quad \textbf{-3y} \qquad\qquad \textbf{-4}$
- $3y^2 + 1y - 4$

You also need to learn how to expand brackets with powers. Powers show how many times a number is multiplied by itself.

EXAMPLE

Expand the bracket $4a^2\ (2a^2 + 6a)$

- $4a^2 \times 2a^2 = 8a^4$

- $4a^2 \times 6a = 24a^3$

- $8a^4 + 24a^3$

You will also need to learn how to expand and simplify expressions.

EXAMPLE 1

Expand and simplify $6(a + 4) - 6$

- $(6 \times a) + (6 \times 4) - 6$
- $6a + 24 - 6$
- $6a + 18$

EXAMPLE 2 - Multiplication Table

Expand the bracket $(h + 6)(3h - 2)$

×	$3h$	-2
h	$3h^2$	$-2h$
6	$18h$	-12

- $3h^2 - 2h + 18h - 12$
- $3h^2 + 16h - 12$

FACTORISATION

Factorising is the process of putting brackets back into expressions.

EXAMPLE 1

Factorise:

$$4y - 8$$

How to factorise:

- First of all, you need to find the highest common factor. This will either be a number or term.
- The common factor will be placed on the outside of the bracket.
- The numbers and terms inside the brackets will be multiplied by the outside term.

DAY 5 ➔ **Algebra**

$4y - 8$

- 4 and 8 are both divisible by 4. So, the number 4 will be placed outside of the brackets.

- Next, you need to work out what you need to multiply by the 4 in order to get the rest of the expression.

$$4(y - 2)$$

If you expand this answer, you should reach the expression we first started with: $4y - 8$.

EXAMPLE 2

Factorise:

$$12ab - 3ac + 6a^2b$$

How to factorise:

- First of all, you need to find the highest common factor. This will either be a number or term.

- The common factor will be placed on the outside of the bracket. The numbers and terms inside the brackets will be multiplied by the outside term.

$12ab - 3ac + 6a^2b$

- The highest common factor of $12ab$, $3ac$ and $6a^2b$ is $3a$.

$$3a(4b - c + 2ab)$$

Activity I

Q1.

1. Factorise:

$$64a^2 - 81b^2$$

2. Factorise:

$$49a^2 - 25b^2$$

3. Expand:

$$-5(5a^2 - 8b^2)$$

4. Expand and simplify:

$$8(2a + 8) + 4(9a - 3)$$

MAKING X THE SUBJECT

Sometimes, you may be required to make x the subject in a formula. The best way to explain this via example.

EXAMPLE

Take a look at the triangle and rectangle below. Both have equal perimeters.

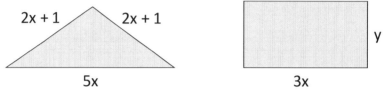

This means that $9x + 2 = 6x + 2y$

To rearrange the formula to make 'x' the subject, you should follow the instructions below:

$(2x + 1) + (2x + 1) + 5x$, simplified to

$2x + 2x + 5x + 1 + 1 = 9x + 2$

Perimeter of the rectangle is:

$3x + 3x + y + y = 6x + 2y$

Perimeter of triangle = Perimeter of rectangle

$9x + 2 = 6x + 2y$

Collect the term x on one side and the rest on the other:

$9x - 6x = 2y - 2$

$3x = 2y - 2$

$x = \dfrac{2y - 2}{3}$

LINEAR EQUATIONS

A **LINEAR EQUATION** is an equation that forms a straight line (if you were to plot the results on a grid).

Below are a couple of examples of linear equations:

- $y = 2x + 1$
- $x = 4x - 2$

You can use number machines to write the rules of an equation. The important thing to remember when using this with regards to algebra, is to use BIDMAS.

X ⟶ +2 ⟶ +5 = 2

You can work out the value of x by working backwards, and doing the opposite to what the number machine is telling you.

2 ⟶ -5 ⟶ -2 = −5

- $x = -5$

SOLVING AND BALANCING EQUATIONS

When we think of an equation, we need to think of a balance beam or balancing scale!

Both sides of an equation must BALANCE. Each expression on either side of the equals sign is representing the same value.

To solve an equation, you will need to work out all of the missing values. There may be more than one missing value.

GOLDEN NUGGETS

1. Whatever you do to one side of the equation, you must do to the other side.

2. Often, you will need to get rid of something on one side, to work out the missing value. To get rid of something, you must do the opposite to what it is saying (if the equation uses a +, you will −. If the equation uses a ÷, you will ×).

3. You will need to keep getting rid of values, until you are left with one letter.

Sometimes you will need to solve an equation with unknowns on both sides.

EXAMPLE 1

Expand the bracket:

$$8(a + 4) = 24a - 16$$

- $8a + 32 = 24a - 16$

- $32 = 16a - 16$

- $48 = 16a$

- $a = 3$

EXAMPLE 2

Solve the equation:

$$\frac{6b + 8}{4} = 9.5$$

- This fraction is basically saying: $6b + 8$ needs to ALL be divided by 4.

- Inverse the operations to solve the equation:

- $6b + 8 = 9.5 \times 4$

- $6b + 8 = 38$

- $6b = 30$

- $b = 5$

Activity 2

Q1.

Simplify the following:

$$2(a + b) \times c \quad = \quad$$

Q2.

Expand the following:

a. $-y(3y + 4)$

b. $5y(x - 4a)$

c. $-4(6a^2 - 5x^2)$

SIMULTANEOUS EQUATIONS

The difference between the equations we have previously worked through, and simultaneous equations, is that simultaneous equations require you to work out two unknown values.

To work out the unknown values, you will need to work out two equations at the same time; finding out what the value of x and y is.

EXAMPLE

Solve the simultaneous equations and work out the value of x and y.

$$2x + y = 14$$

$$4x - y = 16$$

How to work it out:

- $2x + y = 14$... Eq (1)

- $4x - y = 16$... Eq (2)

- Notice that both y has coefficient of 1; $+y$ and $-y$ so we can eliminate y first by Eq (1) + Eq (2)

- $2x + 4x + y - y = 14 + 16$

- $6x = 30$

- $x = 30 \div 6$

- $x = 5$

- Then substitute $x = 5$ into either Eq (1) or Eq (2) to find y

- $2(5) + y = 14$

- $10 + y = 14$

- $y = 14 - 10$

- $y = 4$

FINDING A COMMON COEFFICIENT

A common coefficient is needed in order to work out simultaneous equations. Some equations will contain commonality, whereas others may not.

EXAMPLE

Solve the simultaneous equations and work out the value of × and y.

$$4x + 3y = 55$$

$$3x - 2y = 3$$

How to work it out:

- $4x + 3y = 55$... Eq (1)

- $3x - 2y = 3$... Eq (2)

- We can either make the coefficient of x equal or coefficient of y equal to eliminate. Let's make the coefficient of y equal, we multiplied each term in Eq(1) by 2 and each term in Eq(2) by 3.

- $8x + 6y = 110$... Eq (3)

- $9x - 6y = 9$... Eq(4)

- Adding Eq(3) to Eq (4) to eliminate y

- $8x + 9y + 6y - 6y = 110 + 9$

- $17x = 119$

- $x = 119 \div 17 = 7$

- Then substitute $x = 7$ into either Eq (1) or Eq (2)

- $3(7) - 2y = 3$

- $21 - 2y = 3$

- $21 - 3 = 2y$

- $18 = 2y$

- $y = 18 \div 2$

- $y = 9$

Activity 3

Q1.

Solve the simultaneous equations and work out the value of *a* and *b*.

$$2a + 5b = 33$$
$$a + 3b = 19$$

Q2.

Solve the simultaneous equations and work out the value of *a* and *b*.

$$4a - 6b = 0$$
$$6a + 2b = 22$$

Q3.

Solve the simultaneous equations and work out the value of × and *y*.

$$x + 2y = 22$$
$$-x + 5y = 27$$

Q4.

Solve the simultaneous equations, and work out the value of × and *y*.

$$4x + 2y = 22$$
$$6x - 2y = 28$$

QUADRATIC EQUATIONS

The most general way to write a quadratic equation is like so:

$$ax^2 + bx + c = 0$$

QUADRATIC EQUATIONS contain only terms up to and including x^2. In the above example, you need to remember that a cannot be equal to 0, but the terms b and c can.

QUADRATIC FORMULA

This formula can be used for equations that cannot be factorised. The formula is:

$$x = \frac{-b \pm \sqrt{b^2 - 4ac}}{2a}$$

Example 2 uses the quadratic formula as a way of explaining it further.

EXAMPLE 1

Solve the following quadratic equation:

$$(x + 9)(x - 4) = 0$$

- The product of $x + 9$ and $x - 4$ is 0.

- Therefore either $x + 9 = 0$ OR $x - 4 = 0$.

- $x + 9 = 0$

- $x = -9$

- $x - 4 = 0$

- $x = 4$

- So, $x = -9$ or $x = 4$.

EXAMPLE 2

Solve the following equation using the quadratic formula.

$$x^2 + 8x - 10 = 0$$

- $a = 1 \quad b = 8 \quad c = -10$

$$X = \frac{(-8) \pm \sqrt{8^2 - 4 \times 1 \times (-10)}}{2}$$

$$X = \frac{(-8) \pm \sqrt{64 + 40}}{2}$$

$$X = \frac{(-8) \pm \sqrt{104}}{2}$$

$$X = \frac{(-8) + \sqrt{104}}{2} = 1.10 \ (2 \ d.p.)$$

$$X = \frac{(-8) - \sqrt{104}}{2} = -9.10 \ (2 \ d.p.)$$

Activity 4

Q1.

1. Solve the following quadratic equation:
$$(x + 27)(x - 3) = 0$$

2. Show how you would factorise the following quadratic equation:
$$x^2 - 4x - 12 = 0$$

3. Solve the following quadratic equation:
$$x^2 - 38 = 0$$

INEQUALITIES

As the name suggests, 'inequalities' refers to symbols that do not show EQUAL values.

LEARN YOUR INEQUALITIES!

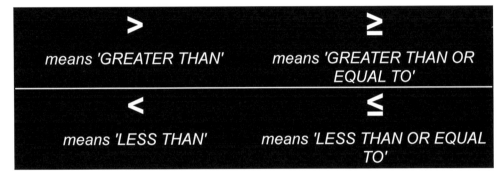

>	≥
means 'GREATER THAN'	*means 'GREATER THAN OR EQUAL TO'*
<	≤
means 'LESS THAN'	*means 'LESS THAN OR EQUAL TO'*

EXAMPLE

$x < 8$ **(in terms of integer possibilities)**

- This means that 'x' is LESS THAN 8.
- The possibilities of the value of x are: 7, 6, 5, 4, 3, 2, 1

$-4 < x \leq 3$ **(in terms of integer possibilities)**

- This means that 'x' is MORE THAN −4. It also means that 'x' is LESS THAN OR EQUAL TO 3.
- The possibilities of the value of x are: −3, −2, −1, 0, 1, 2, 3

A cool way to remember the different symbols...

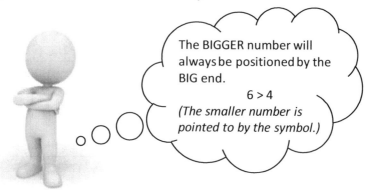

The BIGGER number will always be positioned by the BIG end.

$$6 > 4$$

(The smaller number is pointed to by the symbol.)

Sometimes, you may be required to rearrange the inequality in order to solve it.

EXAMPLE 1

Solve the inequality:

$$4x + 1 < 37$$

How to work it out:

- In order to solve this inequality, you need to begin by getting the x value on its own.

- We can move the '+1' to the other side, which then becomes '-1'.

    $4x < 36$

- To find x, you now need to divide each side by 4:

    $x < 9$

EXAMPLE 2

Solve the inequality:

$$9y - 1 < 53$$

How to work it out:

- In order to solve this inequality, you need to begin by getting the y value on its own.

- We can move the ' -1' to the other side, which then becomes '$+1$'.

  $9y < 54$

- To find y, you now need to divide each side by 9:

  $y < 6$

When working with inequalities, you can also use number lines to represent the same information.

Drawing a number line is really simple! However, there are a few things that you need to remember.

- If you use > or <, you will need to use an **open circle**. An open circle is used because the number is NOT included. ◯

- If you use ≤ or ≥, you will need to use a **coloured-in circle**. A coloured-in circle is used because the number IS included. ●

EXAMPLE 1

$-3 < x \le 2$

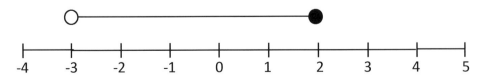

EXAMPLE 2

$-3 \leq x \leq 3$

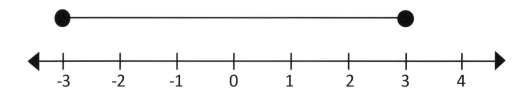

SOLVING INEQUALITIES

Solving inequalities is relatively simple if you have already mastered how to solve equations – it uses the exact same method!

Instead of using an equals sign, you are simply using an inequality sign.

Let us demonstrate this with an example.

EXAMPLE

Solve the inequality:

$$5a + 4 > 11$$

- $5a + 4 > 11$

- You want to move the numbers on one side of the sign and keep the a on the other side.

- $5a > 7$

- $a > 1.4$

- This means that the value of a can be anything that is bigger than (not including) 1.4.

Activity 5

Q1

Based on the number line, write down the inequality for x.

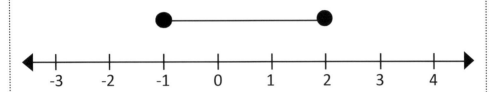

Q2.

Solve the inequality:

$$8(4 - 3x) \leq 10$$

SEQUENCES

A number sequence is a sequence of numbers that follow a rule.

There are lots of different number patterns that you should familiarise yourselves with, and these include the following:

- Even and odd numbers;
- Prime numbers;
- Square numbers;
- Cube numbers;
- Triangle numbers;
- Multiples.

LINEAR SEQUENCES

A linear sequence is a number pattern which increases or decreases by the SAME AMOUNT each time.

How to work out the rule of a linear sequence:

- The secret to working out the rule of a linear sequence is to work out what you have to do to get from one number to the next.

- Once you think you have found the rule, double check that it works for the rest of the sequence.

- Generally, there are two types of linear sequence to look out for:

ADDING THE SAME NUMBER

Number sequences may be progressing by <u>adding</u> the <u>same number</u>.

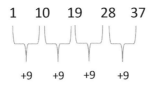

SUBTRACTING THE SAME NUMBER

Number sequences may be progressing by <u>subtracting</u> the <u>same number</u>.

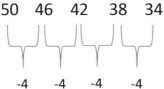

MULTIPLYING OR DIVIDING BY THE SAME NUMBER

Number sequences may be progressing by <u>multiplying</u> or <u>dividing</u> by the <u>same number</u>.

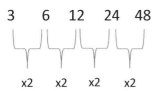

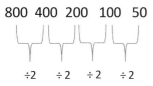

DAY 5 ➡ **Algebra**

FINDING THE Nᵀᴴ TERM

Sometimes, you may be asked questions on sequences that asks you to find the 100th value.

Of course, you are not going to sit there and work out the values for every number from 1 to 100. You need a quick way to work out the value.

There is a simple method to work out the nth term of a sequence, so long as you know the common difference.

EXAMPLE

Find an expression for the nth term of the following sequence:

4   7   10   13   16

How to work it out:

1. First of all, you need to find the common difference. The sequence is progressing by adding 3. So, in the formula you would write $3n$. 'n' is the term you are trying to work out.

n	1	2	3	4	5
term	4	7	10	13	16

2. Next, you need to list the values of $3n$.

3	6	9	12

$(3 + 1) = 4$ $(6 + 1) = 7$ $(9 + 1) = 10$ $(12 + 1) = 13$

3. Work out what you have to do to get from $3n$ to each term. As you can see, you need to add 1.

So, the formula is $3n + 1$.

Some questions may ask you whether a value would appear in the sequence.

You can work out whether the value would appear in the sequence by equating the value to the nth term expression and solving the resulting equation to work out the value of n.

If n is a whole number, the value **WOULD** appear in the sequence. If n is a decimal or fraction of a number, the value would **NOT** appear in the sequence.

EXAMPLE

Using the rule $4n + 2$, work out whether the term 22 appears in the sequence.

How to work it out:

1. Let's use the rule and place 22 after the equals sign:

    $4n + 2 = 22$

2. That means $4n = 20$. So you need to work out the value of one n.

    $20 \div 4 = 5$

    $n = 5$

3. The value of n is a whole number, which means that 22 **WOULD** appear in this sequence. 22 is the 5th value of the sequence.

REMEMBER TO USE COMMON SENSE!

Sometimes, you can work out whether a number is going to appear in a sequence based on all of the other numbers in the sequence.

For example, if all of the values in the sequence are even, that means an odd number is not going to appear in the sequence.

Another example, if all the values end in 2 or 7, that means a number ending in 1 is not going to appear in the sequence.

QUADRATIC SEQUENCES

A quadratic sequence is when the difference between each value is not constant. It becomes a quadratic sequence if the second difference is the same.

The best way to get your head around quadratic sequences is via an example.

EXAMPLE

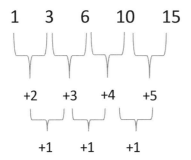

- As you can see, the <u>first difference</u> between each term changes each time.

- However, when looking at the difference, you should realise that these differences are increasing by 1 each time. This is the <u>second difference</u>.

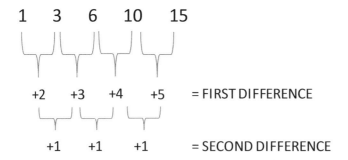

FINDING THE Nᵀᴴ TERM

Finding the nth term of a quadratic sequence is a little bit more tricky than linear sequences.

EXAMPLE

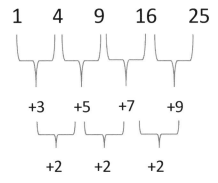

- As you can see, the numbers in the sequence are squared numbers.
- The nth term of this sequence is n^2.

Activity 6

1. Which two numbers come next in the sequence?

2   4   8   16   32   64

A	B	C	D
126 215	128 256	128 265	182 265

2. Below are four match sticks.

Pattern 1

The pattern continues as follows:

Pattern 1   **Pattern 2**   **Pattern 3**

a) How many match sticks would be in pattern 9?

b) If *m* represents the number of match sticks, and *p* represents the pattern number, write the rule to work out how the sequence is progressing.

3. The rule you are given is $7n + 9$.

If *n* represents the nth term in the sequence, what would the 35th term in the sequence be?

ANSWERS TO DAY 5

EXPRESSIONS AND FORMS

ACTIVITY I

Q1.

1) $(8a - 9b)(8a + 9b)$

- Both 64 and 81 are square numbers.
- $(8a)^2 + (9b)^2$
- $(8a - 9b)(8a + 9b)$

2) $(7a - 5b)(7a + 5b)$

- Both 49 and 25 are square numbers.
- $(7a)^2 - (5b)^2$
- $(7a - 5b)(7a + 5b)$

3) $-25a^2 + 40b^2$

- $-5 \times 5a^2 = -25a^2$
- $-5 \times -8b^2 = 40b^2$
- $-25a^2 + 40b^2$

4) $52a + 52$

- $16a + 64 + 36a - 12$

- $16a + 36a = 52a$

- $64 - 12 = 52$

- $52a + 52$

LINEAR EQUATIONS

ACTIVITY 2

Q1.

2) $2(a + b) \times c = (2a + 2b) \times c = 2ac + 2bc$

Q2.

a) $-3y^2 - 4y$

b) $5yx - 20ya$

c) $-24a^2 + 20x^2$

SIMULTANEOUS EQUATIONS

ACTIVITY 3

Q1.

$a = 4 \quad b = 5$

- $2a + 5b = 33$
- $a + 3b = 19 \ (2a + 6b = 38)$
- $2a + 5b = 33$
- $2a + 6b = 38$

$b = 5$

- $(5 \times 5) + 2a = 33$
- $25 + 2a = 33$
- $33 - 25 = 8 \ (8 \div 2 = 4)$

$a = 4$

Q2.

$a = 3 \quad b = 2$

- $4a - 6b = 0 \ (\times 3)$
- $6a - 2b = 22 \ (\times 2)$
- $12a + 18b = 0$
- $12a + 4b = 44$
- $22b = 44$

$b = 2$

- $4a - (6 \times 2) = 0$
- $4a - 12 = 0$
- $(4 \times 3) - 12 = 0$

$a = 3$

Q3.

$x = 8 \qquad y = 7$

- $x + 2y = 22$
- $-x + 5y = 27$
- $7y = 49$

$y = 7$

- $(2 \times 7) + x = 22$
- $14 + x = 22$

$x = 8$

Q4.

$x = 5 \qquad y = 1$

- Eliminate y
- $10x = 50$

$x = 5$

- $(4 \times 5) + 2y = 22$
- $22 + (2 \times 1) = 22$

$y = 1$

QUADRATIC EQUATIONS

ACTIVITY 4

Q1.

$x = 3$ or $x = -27$

- Begin by simplifying both sides of the equation: $x^2 + 24x - 81 = 0$
- Use quadratic formula with $a = 1$, $b = 24$, $c = -81$

Q2.

$(x + 2)(x - 6)$

- Solve by finding two numbers with a product of -12 and a sum of -4. This is $+2 \times -6$ as this equals -12.

Q3.

$x = \sqrt{38}$ or $x = -\sqrt{38}$

$x^2 - 38 = 0$

$x^2 = 38$

$x = \pm\sqrt{38}$

INEQUALITIES

ACTIVITY 5

Q1.

$-1 \leq x \leq 2$

Q2.

$x \geq 11/12$

$$\frac{8(4-3x)}{8} \leq \frac{10}{8}$$

$$4 - 3x \leq \frac{5}{4}$$

$$4 - 3x - 4 \leq \frac{5}{4} - 4$$

$$-3x \leq \frac{11}{4} = 3x \geq \frac{11}{4}$$

$$3x \geq \frac{11}{4}$$

$$x \geq \frac{11}{12}$$

SEQUENCES

ACTIVITY 6

Q1.

B = 128, 256

- The pattern sees the previous number doubled.

Q2.

a) 28

- The number of match sticks is increasing by 3 each.
- To work out the ninth pattern:

    $9 \times 3 = 27 + 1 = 28$

b) number of match sticks (m) = number pattern (p × 3) + 1

Q3.

254

- $7 \times 35 + 9 = 254$

Day 5 Checklist

You have now completed your Day 5 revision.

How confident are you feeling?

Below we have included a checklist that you can tick off to make sure that you have learnt everything regarding this chapter.

I have read and understood the examples for tackling different Algebra calculations.

I have tackled all of the questions in this section.

I have read and understood the answers in this section.

I feel confident in Algebra questions.

EXAM PRACTICE 1
Day 6

Answer ALL questions.
Write your answers in the spaces provided.

1 (a) Write the following numbers in order of size, starting with the smallest.

0.3   30   0.03   0.31   30.1

....

(1 mark)

(b) Write the following numbers in order of size, starting with the biggest.

103   25   50   55   101

....

(1 mark)

(c) Write the following numbers in order of size, starting with the smallest.

25%   0.5   ⅕   75%   0.1

....

(1 mark)

2 Katie is given weekly pocket money for her part-time jobs. Here is how much she earns across six weeks.

£40.60   £32.20   £75.80   £25.00   £15.50   £20.90

(a) Work out the mean.

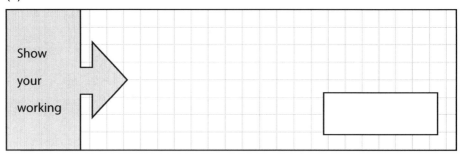

Show your working

(2 marks)

DAY 6 ➡ **Exam Practice 1**

(b) In week 7, Katie earns £70.30. How much does Katie have altogether?

....

....

(2 marks)

(c) Katie's friend Sarah earns 20% more than Katie's total earnings.

Work out how much Sarah earns.

Show

your

working

(2 marks)

3 (a) Convert 75% to its simplest fraction.

....

....

(2 marks)

(b) Work out which is the greater value:

60% of 950

Or

⅗ of 1,000

Explain your answer.

....

....

(2 marks)

4   Below is a 6-sided polygon.

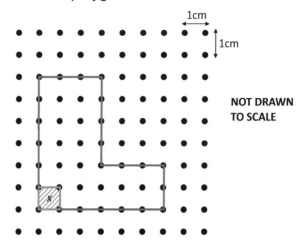

NOT DRAWN
TO SCALE

(a) Write down the mathematical term for a 6-sided shape.

....

(1 mark)

(b) Write down the mathematical term for the angle marked x.

....

(1 mark)

(c) On the diagram above, mark with arrows ⟫ one pair of parallel lines.

(1 mark)

(d) What is the area of the 6-sided polygon?

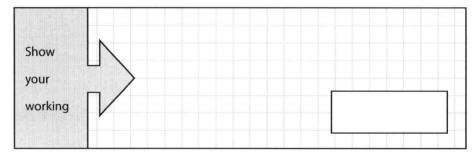

Show

your

working

(2 marks)

DAY 6 ➡   **Exam Practice 1**

5 (a) What fraction of the shape is shaded?

Write your answer in its simplest form.

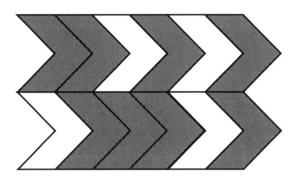

....

(1 mark)

(b) Shade in the other half so that the line becomes a line of symmetry.

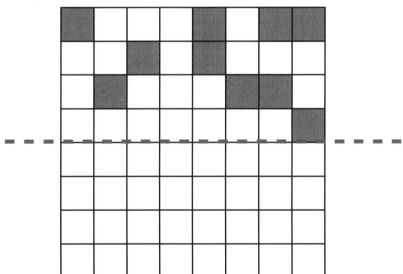

(2 marks)

6   The pictogram below represents the number of star jumps each person could do in a one minute period. Each person attempted their star jumps three times.

Using the information provided, create a chart or diagram which allows you to compare each person's results.

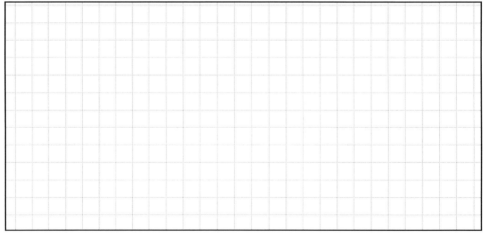

(5 marks)

7 (a) Simplify the following fraction.

$\dfrac{40}{68}$

Give your answer in its simplest form.

....

(1 mark)

(b) Write $\dfrac{2}{5}$ as a decimal.

....

(1 mark)

(c) India says that $\dfrac{3}{7}$ is bigger than $\dfrac{2}{3}$.

Is she right?

Explain your answer.

....

....

....

....

....

(2 marks)

8   The diagram shows a circle.

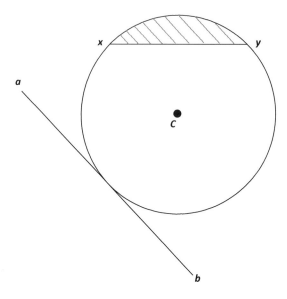

(a) What is the mathematical term for line xy?

....

(1 mark)

(b) Measure the length of the radius, in millimetres, of the circle.

....

(1 mark)

(c) What is the mathematical term for the line ab?

....

(1 mark)

(d) Measure the length of the diameter, in millimetres, of the circle.

....

(1 mark)

9 Below are three different offers for a 49-inch plasma TV.

Online Store 1

SPECIAL OFFER

Original price =
£268.00

Discount =
20% off!

Online Store 2

SPECIAL OFFER

Original price =
£295.00

Discount =
$\frac{1}{4}$ off!

Online Store 3

SPECIAL OFFER

Pay £18.50
weekly for 16
weeks

Work out which online store offers the cheapest deal.

You must show ALL of your working out.

....

....

....

....

....

....

....

....

....

(6 marks)

10 The bar chart below shows the number of people who applied for a Sales Assistant job.

The job was advertised for one week, and the bars on the chart represent each day of the week up until the closing date.

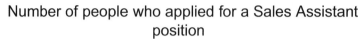

Number of people who applied for a Sales Assistant position

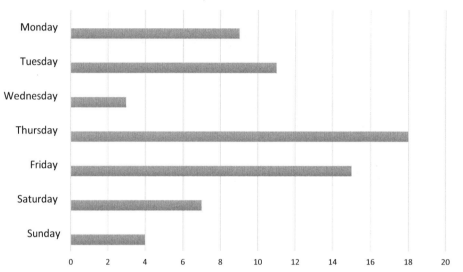

Work out how many people applied for the Sales Assistant position overall.

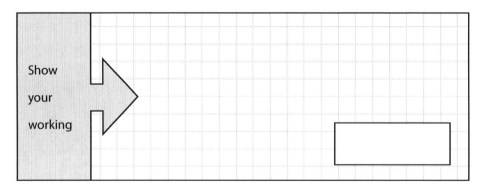

Show your working

(2 marks)

EXAM PRACTICE 1
(Non-Calculator)

1. (a) 0.03, 0.3, 0.31, 30, 30.1	1 mark
Pay attention to where the decimal point is. It can be confusing because some of the numbers only have 2 digits, whereas some have 3. You can always add a '0' to the end of the digits, so that all of the decimals contain the same amount of digits: 0.03 0.30 0.31 30.0 30.1	
1. (b) 103, 101, 55, 50, 25	1 mark
Be sure to pay attention to what the question is asking you. This is a simple question, but it is asking you to write the numbers starting with the BIGGEST.	Award no marks if answer is written from smallest to biggest.
1. (c) 0.1, ⅕, 25%, 0.5, 75%	1 mark

Convert the numbers all into percentages to work out the order of size.
 	
   0.1 = 10%
   ⅕ = 20%
   25%
   0.5 = 50%	

75%	2 marks
2. (a) £35.00	(1 mark for adding up the total amount).
To work out the mean:	(1 mark for correctly dividing by how many numbers there are).
$\quad\quad$ 40.60	
$\quad\quad$ 32.20	
$\quad\quad$ 75.80	
$\quad\quad$ 25.00	
$\quad\quad$ 15.50	
+ $\quad$ 20.90	
$\quad\quad$ 210.00	
210 ÷ 6 = 35	2 marks
2. (b) £280.30	(1 mark for having the correct total across the first 6 weeks).
In week 7, Katie earns £70.30. In total, she has:	(1 mark for correctly adding both amounts).
$\quad\quad$ 210.00	
+ $\quad$ 70.30	2 marks
$\quad\quad$ 280.30	
	(1 mark for working out 20% of Katie's earnings)
2. (c) £336.36	
Katie's earnings £280.30	(1 mark for adding Katie's earnings with the 20%).
Sarah earns 20% more.	
$\quad$ 10% of 280.30 = 28.03	
$\quad$ 20% = 28.03 + 28.03 = 56.06	
So Sarah earns 280.30 + 56.06 = 336.36	2 marks
	(1 mark for converting it to a fraction).
3. (a) ¾	
75% as a fraction = 75 over 100 = $^{75}/_{100}$	(1 mark for the answer being written in its simplest form).
Both of these numbers can be divided by 25 to simplify it to: ¾.	

3. (b) ⅗ of 1,000 is the greater value.

60% of 950 = 950 ÷ 100 = 9.5

9.5 × 60 = 570.

⅗ of 1000 = 1000 ÷ 5 = 200

200 × 3 = 600.

Therefore ⅗ of 1000 is the greater value.

2 marks

(1 mark for working out each part of the calculation).

4. (a) hexagon

A six-sided shape is a hexagon.

1 mark

4. (b) right angle

An angle at 90° is a right angle.

1 mark

4. (c) You could have marked the following parallel lines:

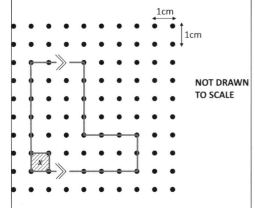

NOT DRAWN TO SCALE

1 mark

(You could have also marked the two vertical sides. Parallel lines are lines that are the same distance apart and are not touching).

4. (d) 24 cm²

2 marks

(1 mark for the correct answer).

(1 mark for showing how you calculated the correct answer).

The 6 sided shape is drawn on a 1x1 grid which means each square represents 1cm. The shape covers 24 squares, so this is the area.

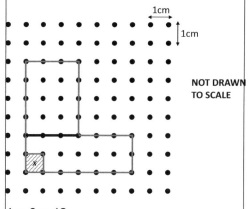

NOT DRAWN TO SCALE

4 × 3 = 12

2 × 6 = 12

12 + 12 = 24 cm²

5. (a) ⅔

1 mark

(Award no marks if the fraction has not been simplified).

8 of the arrows are shaded. There are 12 arrows in total. Therefore the fraction of shaded arrows is ⁸⁄₁₂.

Both numbers can be divided by 4, to simplify it to: ⅔.

5. (b) Your answer should look like this:

2 marks

(Award 2 marks for all correct squares shaded in. Only award 1 mark if one of the squares has been shaded in incorrectly. Award 0 marks if more than 1 square has been shaded in incorrectly).

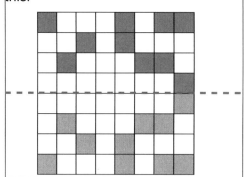

6. You need to draw a chart to compare the results. A bar chart or frequency table would be a great way to compare each of their results.

Your chart could look something like this:

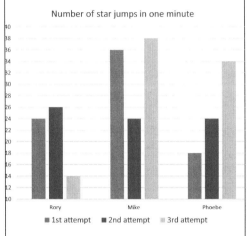

Number of star jumps in one minute

■ 1st attempt   ■ 2nd attempt   ▨ 3rd attempt

5 marks

(Award the five marks for the correct data inserted into a graph that compares all three people's results, with each of their attempts).

7. (a) $^{10}/_{17}$

$^{40}/_{68}$ = both numbers can be divided by 4.

1 mark

7. (b) 0.4

$^{2}/_{5}$ as a decimal:

$2 \div 5 = 0.4$

You could also work it out like so:

$100 \div 5 = 20 \times 2 = 40\%$

$40 \div 100 = 0.4$

1 mark

1 mark

7. (c) India is not right. $\frac{3}{7}$ is not bigger than $\frac{2}{3}$.	2 marks
	(1 mark for correct answer).
You need to change the denominator so that they are both the same.	(1 mark for quality of written communication demonstrated in workings out).
The denominator '7' and '3' can be changed to the same denominator, which in this case is '21' (both numbers can go into 21).	
$\frac{3}{7} = \frac{9}{21}$	
$\frac{2}{3} = \frac{14}{21}$	
8. (a) Chord	1 mark
8. (b) 26.5 mm	1 mark
8. (c) Tangent	1 mark
8. (d) 53 mm	1 mark
9. Online Store 1 offers the cheapest deal	6 marks
	(Award 2 marks for correct answer).
Online Store 1 = 20% off £268.00	(Award 1 mark for attempt of showing working out).
10% = 26.80	
20% = 26.80 + 26.80 = 53.60	(Award 1 mark for correct working out to online store 1).
268.00 − 53.60 = £214.40	
Online Store 2 = ¼ off £295	(Award 1 mark for correct working out to online store 2).
295 ÷ 4 = 73.75	
295 − 73.75 = £221.25	(Award 1 mark for correct working out to online store 3).
Online Store 3 = £18.50 for 16 weeks	
18.50 × 16 = £296	
Therefore Online Store 1 offers the best deal.	

10. 67 people applied for the job	2 marks

Each line on the graph represents '2'.
  Monday = 9
  Tuesday = 11
  Wednesday = 3
  Thursday = 18
  Friday = 15
  Saturday = 7
  Sunday = 4
 	
  9 + 11 + 3 + 18 + 15 + 7 + 4 = 67
	(Award 1 mark for correct answer)
	(Award 1 mark for correctly interpreting the data).

Day 6 Checklist

You have now completed your Day 6 revision.

How confident are you feeling?

Below we have included a checklist that you can tick off to make sure that you have learnt everything regarding this chapter.

I have practised all of the exam questions in this chapter.

I have tried working under similar exam conditions (timing and no distractions etc.)

I have read and understood the answers in this section.

I feel confident in my Maths GCSE.

EXAM PRACTICE 2
Day 7

Answer ALL questions.
Write your answers in the spaces provided.

1. Estimate the answer to the calculation below. You must show your working.

$$\frac{4805 \times 0.213}{5.236 + 4.721}$$

....

....

....

(3 marks)

2. (a) (i) Insert brackets to make this calculation easier to read.

$$4 \times 12 \div 3 = 16$$

(1 mark)

(ii) Insert brackets to make this calculation correct.

$$2 \times 30 - 14 = 32$$

(1 mark)

(iii) Andy says that $4 \times 3 - 2 \times 7 = -2$

Ryan says the answer to this calculation is 70.

Who is correct, and explain your reasons why.

....

....

....

(2 marks)

3. The diagram below shows the landscape of a field. The area of
    the landscape is 188 m².

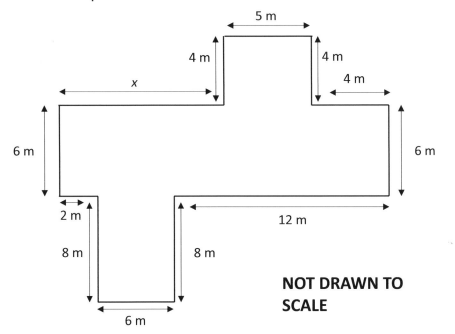

Work out the value of x.

NOT DRAWN TO SCALE

....

(2 marks)

4. (a) Write the following number in standard form:

524,000

....

(a)..

(1 mark)

(b) What is 0.000008 in standard form?

....

....

....

(b)..

(2 marks)

(c) Calculate the following

$(5.5 \times 10^7) - (3.14 \times 10^4)$

Give your answer in standard form.

....

....

....

(c)..

(2 marks)

5. Tessa, Holly and Julie have a bag of counters.

There are 8 orange, 10 yellow and 6 pink counters in the bag.

(a) What is the probability of picking a counter that is either orange or pink?

. . . .

(a). . . . .

(1 mark)

(b) Tessa says, "I don't want any orange counters".

What is the probability of Tessa picking a colour that she wants?

. . . .

(b). . . . .

(1 mark)

(c) What is the fraction of pink counters out of the total of counters in the bag? Give your answer in its simplest form.

. . . .

(c). . . . .

(1 mark)

(d) 6 more counters are added into the bag. These counters are 2 different colours to what's already in the bag. There are now 5 colours in the bag. What is the probability of picking a new colour counter from the bag?

. . . .

(d). . . . .

(1 mark)

6. The below table and histogram show information about the number of times pupils arrived late to school. The study is out of 136 people.

Mark (n%)	Frequency
0 < n ≤ 2	10
2 < n ≤ 3	18
3 < n ≤ 5	
5 < n ≤ 6	30
6 < n ≤ 7	
7 < n ≤ 10	30

(a) Use the table above to complete the histogram.

(2 marks)

(b) Use the histogram to complete the table.

(2 marks)

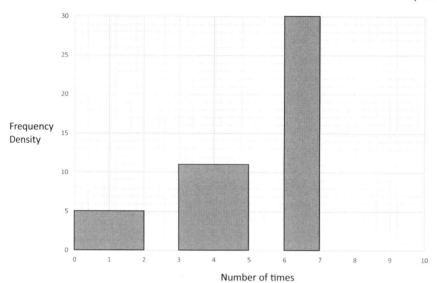

DAY 7 ➡ **Exam Practice 2**

7. David is the Operations Manager of a book publishing company.

   He is conducting self-evaluations with each team member. There are 8 employees who David must spend time with.

   These self-evaluations need to be completed in a 5 hour period, with a short break of 10 minutes between each person. Each person will be self-evaluated individually.

   (a) Work out the maximum amount of time David can spend on each person's self-evaluation. Give your answer to the nearest minute.

   ....

   ....

   ....

   ....

   (a)..

   (3 marks)

   (b) Michael is saving money to buy his first house. Currently, Michael has £3,800 in his bank account. His bank account pays 5% compound interest each year.

   (i) How much money will Michael have after 2 years?

   ....

   ....

   (b) (i)..

   (1 mark)

   (ii) How many years will it take Michael to reach over £5,000?

   ....

   (b) (ii)..

   (2 marks)

DAY 7 ➡ **Exam Practice 2**

8. (a) Below is a semi-circle which has a diameter of 32 cm.

Work out the perimeter of the semi-circle.

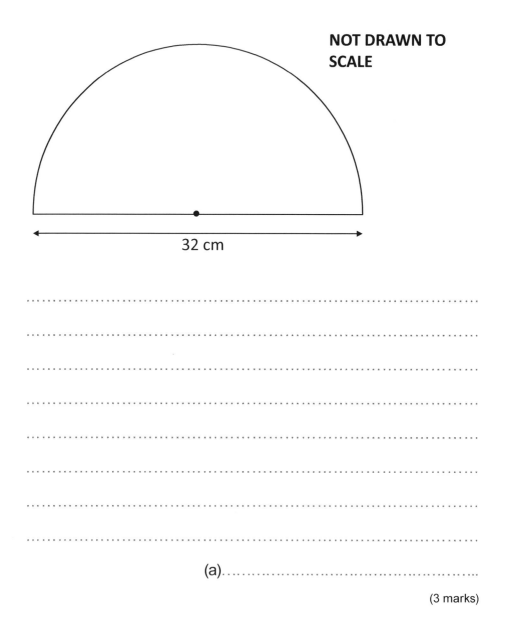

NOT DRAWN TO SCALE

32 cm

....

....

....

....

....

....

....

....

(a)...

(3 marks)

(b) Below is a circle.

Find the circumference and the area.

NOT DRAWN TO SCALE

6 cm

(i) Circumference =

....

....

....

....

(i)..

(2 marks)

(ii) Area =

....

....

....

....

(ii)..

(2 marks)

DAY 7 ➡ **Exam Practice 2**

9. (a) AB and CD are parallel straight lines.

Work out the value of x.

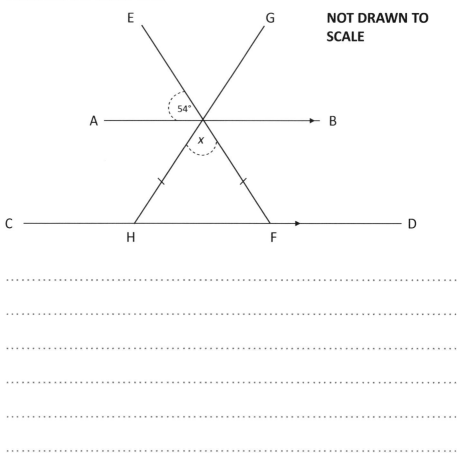

NOT DRAWN TO SCALE

....

....

....

....

....

....

....

(a)..

(3 marks)

(b) Lines AB and CD are parallel.

Work out the value of x.

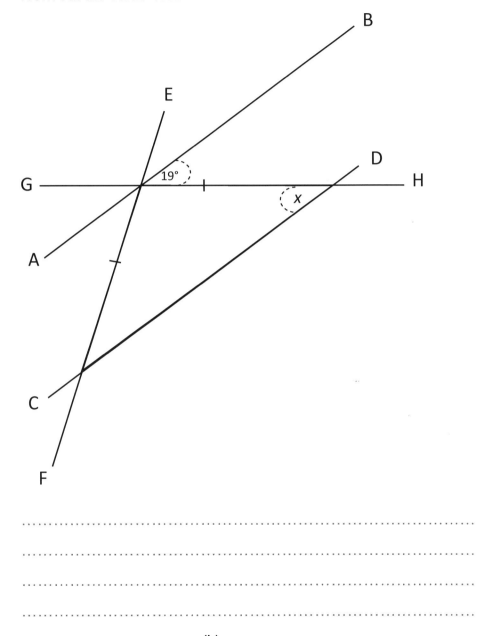

....

....

....

....

(b)..

(2 marks)

10. (a) A scale of a map is 1 cm : 30,000 cm. A distance is measured as 4 cm on the map.

How many centimetres, metres and kilometres is this equivalent to based on the scale of the map?

(i) Centimetres =

....

....

(i)..

(1 mark)

(ii) Metres =

....

....

(ii)..

(1 mark)

(iii) Kilometres =

....

....

(iii)..

(1 mark)

EXAM PRACTICE 2
(Non-Calculator)

1. 100	3 marks
Estimations = 5,000 × 0.200 = 1,000	(2 marks for rounding the numbers up).
5.3 + 4.7 = 10	(1 mark for estimation being ± 10).
1,000 ÷ 10 = 100	
Q2. (a) (i) 4 × (12 ÷ 3) = 16 or (4 × 12) ÷ 3 = 16	1 mark
Q2. (a) (ii) 2 × (30 − 14) = 32	1 mark
You need to subtract 14 from 30, before multiplying by 2.	
Q2 (a) (iii) Andy is correct. You need to do multiplication before subtraction.	2 marks
	(1 mark for correct answer).
	(1 mark for explanation).
4 × 3 = 12	
2 × 7 = 14	
12 − 14 = -2	
Q3. 11 m	2 marks
12 + 6 + 2 = 20 metres is the total length.	(1 mark for correct answer).
	(1 mark for showing working out).
Therefore 20 − 4 − 5 = 11 (you subtract the lengths you already know, in order to work out the missing length).	

Q4. (a) 5.24×10^5 Move the decimal point between the 5 and 2 = 5.24000 Count how many places the decimal point needs to be moved back to reach its original place = 5. So, $524,000 = 5.24 \times 10^5$	1 mark
Q4 (b) 8×10^{-6} $0.000008 = 8 \times 0.000001$ 8×10^{-6}	2 marks (1 mark for correct answer). (1 mark for showing working out).
Q4 (c) 5.49686×10^7 $55,000,000 - 31,400$ $54,968,600$ $= 5.49686 \times 10^7$	2 marks (1 mark for correct answer). (1 mark for showing working out).
Q5 (a) $\frac{7}{12}$. There are 8 orange counters. There are 6 pink counters. There are 24 counters in total. So, 8 + 6 = 14.	1 mark
Q5 (b) $\frac{2}{3}$. If Tessa does not want an orange counter, that means the probability of picking a colour she does want = 10 + 6 = 16 out of a total of 24.	1 mark
Q5 (c) $\frac{1}{4}$ Number of pink counters = 6 out of 24. $\frac{6}{24}$ in its simplest form $\frac{1}{4}$ (both numbers are divisible by 6). Q5 (d) $\frac{1}{5}$.	1 mark 1 mark

If 6 more counters are added, that means there are now 30 counters in total. Instead of 3 colours, the counters are now 5 different colours, which means there are 6 chances of picking a new colour.

Q6. (a) The bar for (2-3 times) should reach 18. The bar for (5-6 times) should reach 30. The bar for (7-10 times) should reach 10.

2 marks

(2 marks for all correct bars. 1 mark for only two of the three bars

Q6 (b) The first missing gap in the table should be 22. The second missing gap should be 30.

2 marks

(1 mark for each correct answer).

Q7 (a) 29 minutes

There are 8 people to perform self-evaluations for. There is a 10 minute interval between each = 70 minutes (1 hour and 10 minutes).

The self-evaluations need to be completed within 5 hours = 5 hours − 1 hour and 10 minutes = 3 hours and 50 minutes (230 minutes).

$230 \div 8 = 28.75$

To the nearest minute = 29.

3 marks

(1 mark for correct answer)

(1 mark for working out the minutes between each individual and subtracting it by the overall total).

(1 mark for dividing minutes by number of people).

Q7 (b) (i) £4189.50

$3,800 \div 100 \times 105 = 3990$

$3990 \div 100 \times 105 = 4189.50$

1 mark

Q7 (b) (ii) 6 years

$3,800 \div 100 \times 105 = 3990 = 1$ year
$3990 \div 100 \times 105 = 4189.5 = 2$ years
$4189 \div 100 \times 105 = 4398.45 = 3$ years
$4398 \div 100 \times 105 = 4617.90 = 4$ years
$4617 \div 100 \times 105 = 4847.85 = 5$ years
$4847 \div 100 \times 105 = 5089.35 = 6$ years

2 marks

(1 mark for correct answer).

(1 mark for working out each year).

Q8 (a) 82.27cm $32 \times \pi = 100.53$ $100.53 \div 2 = 50.265$ $50.265 + 32 = 82.265$ Rounded to 2 dp = 82.27cm	3 marks (1 mark for correct answer). (1 mark for working out circumference). (1 mark for showing all working out with no more than one error).
Q8 (b) (i) 37.7cm $\pi \times 12 = 37.69911184...$ Rounded to 1 dp = 37.7cm	2 marks (1 mark for correct answer). (1 mark for showing correct formula for circumference of a circle).
Q8 (b) (ii) 113.1cm² $\pi \times 6^2 = 113.097335529...$ Rounded to 1 dp = 113.1cm²	2 marks (1 mark for correct answer). (1 mark for correct formula for area of a circle).
Q9 (a) x = 72° $180 - 54 - 54 = 72$	3 marks (1 mark for correct answer) (2 marks for showing workings out of other angles to reach angle x).
Q9 (b) x = 19° Lines AB and CD are parallel. This means the angle of 19° is equivalent to angle x.	2 marks (1 mark for correct answer) (1 marks for showing workings out of other angles to reach angle x).
Q10 (a) (i) 120,000 centimetres $4 \times 30,000 = 120,000$	1 mark
Q10 (a) (ii) 1200 metres $120,000 \div 100 = 1200$	1 mark
Q10 (a) (iii) 1.2 kilometres	1 mark

Day Checklist

You have now completed your Day 7 revision.

How confident are you feeling?

Below we have included a checklist that you can tick off to make sure that you have learnt everything regarding this chapter.

I have practised all of the exam questions in this chapter.

I have tried working under similar exam conditions (timing and no distractions etc.)

I have read and understood the answers in this section.

I feel confident in my Maths GCSE.

DAY 7 ➡ **Checklist**

IMPROVE YOUR MATHEMATICAL ABILITY!

Our How2Become Maths revision guides are the ULTIMATE revision resources to prepare you fully for your Maths GCSE.

Each guide is packed full of examples and practice questions, to ensure that you make the most out of your revision time and can aim to achieve 100%!

FOR MORE INFORMATION ON OUR GCSE GUIDES, PLEASE CHECK OUT THE FOLLOWING:

WWW.HOW2BECOME.COM

FURTHER YOUR LEARNING!

How2Become have created these FANTASTIC guides to help you fully prepare for GCSE languages – French and Spanish with ease!

Take a look at our 'Achieve 100%' series. Improve your learning with the help of these proven study resources.

WWW.HOW2BECOME.COM

Get Access To

FREE

GCSE
TEST QUESTIONS

www.MyEducationalTests.co.uk